P9-APP-369

Social Responsibilities

# of Business Corporations

A Statement on National Policy
by the Research and Policy Committee
of the Committee for Economic Development
June 1971

F.T.S U AT TEXARKANA

9€912

Single Copy . . . $1.50

Printed in U.S.A.
First Printing June 1971
Second Printing April 1972
Third Printing January 1975
Fourth Printing April 1976
Design: Harry Carter
Library of Congress Catalog Card Number: 76-168378
International Standard Book Number: 0-87186-042-2

Committee for Economic Development
477 Madison Avenue, New York, N.Y. 10022

Contents

96912

THE RESPONSIBILITY FOR
CED STATEMENTS ON NATIONAL POLICY

This statement has been approved for publication as a statement of the Research and Policy Committee by the members of that Committee and its drafting sub-committee, subject to individual dissents or reservations noted herein. The trustees who are responsible for this statement are listed on the opposite page. Company associations are included for identification only; the companies do not share in the responsibility borne by the individuals.

The Research and Policy Committee is directed by CED's bylaws to:

"Initiate studies into the principles of business policy and of public policy which will foster the full contribution by industry and commerce to the attainment and maintenance of high and secure standards of living for people in all walks of life through maximum employment and high productivity in the domestic economy."

The bylaws emphasize that:

"All research is to be thoroughly objective in character, and the approach in each instance is to be from the standpoint of the general welfare and not from that of any special political or economic group."

The Research and Policy Committee is composed of 50 Trustees from among the 200 businessmen and educators who comprise the Committee for Economic Development. It is aided by a Research Advisory Board of leading economists, a small permanent Research Staff, and by advisors chosen for their competence in the field being considered.

Each Statement on National Policy is preceded by discussions, meetings, and exchanges of memoranda, often stretching over many months. The research is undertaken by a subcommittee, with its advisors, and the full Research and Policy Committee participates in the drafting of findings and recommendations.

Except for the members of the Research and Policy Committee and the responsible subcommittee, the recommendations presented herein are not necessarily endorsed by other Trustees or by the advisors, contributors, staff members, or others associated with CED.

The Research and Policy Committee offers these Statements on National Policy as an aid to clearer understanding of the steps to be taken in achieving sustained growth of the American economy. The Committee is not attempting to pass on any pending specific legislative proposals; its purpose is to urge careful consideration of the objectives set forth in the statement and of the best means of accomplishing those objectives.

4.

RESEARCH AND POLICY COMMITTEE

Co-Chairmen

EMILIO G. COLLADO, Executive Vice President
Standard Oil Company (New Jersey)

PHILIP M. KLUTZNICK, Chairman
Urban Investment and Development Company

Vice Chairmen

HOWARD C. PETERSEN, Chairman
The Fidelity Bank — *National Economy*

JOHN L. BURNS, President
John L. Burns and Company — *Education and Social & Urban Development*

JOHN A. PERKINS
Graduate School of Management
Northwestern University — *Improvement of Management in Government*

WILLIAM M. ROTH
San Francisco, California — *International Economy*

JERVIS J. BABB
New York, New York

3 JOSEPH W. BARR
President
American Security and Trust Co.

FREDERICK S. BEEBE
Chairman of the Board
Newsweek

S. CLARK BEISE
President (Retired)
Bank of America N.T. & S.A.

WILLIAM BENTON
Publisher and Chairman
Encyclopaedia Britannica, Inc.

1 JOSEPH L. BLOCK
Chairman, Executive Committee
Inland Steel Company

1 MARVIN BOWER, Director
McKinsey & Company, Inc.

JOHN L. BURNS, President
John L. Burns and Company

RAFAEL CARRION, JR.
Chairman and President
Banco Popular de Puerto Rico

EMILIO G. COLLADO
Executive Vice President
Standard Oil Company (New Jersey)

ROBERT C. COSGROVE
Chairman of the Board
Green Giant Company

MARION B. FOLSOM
Rochester, New York

WILLIAM C. FOSTER
Washington, D.C.

JOHN M. FOX, Chairman
United Fruit Company

DAVID L. FRANCIS, Chairman
Princess Coal Sales Company

WILLIAM H. FRANKLIN, President
Caterpillar Tractor Co.

1 RICHARD C. GERSTENBERG
Vice Chairman of the Board
General Motors Corporation

ELLISON L. HAZARD
Chairman and President
Continental Can Company, Inc.

H. J. HEINZ, II, Chairman
H. J. Heinz Company

1 CHARLES KELLER, JR., President
Keller Construction Corporation

2 ROBERT J. KLEBERG, JR., President
King Ranch, Inc.

PHILIP M. KLUTZNICK, Chairman
Urban Investment and Development Co.

RALPH LAZARUS, Chairman
Federated Department Stores, Inc.

1 THOMAS B. McCABE
Chairman, Finance Committee
Scott Paper Company

1 GEORGE C. McGHEE
Washington, D.C.

RAYMON H. MULFORD, Chairman
Owens-Illinois Inc.

1 ROBERT R. NATHAN, President
Robert R. Nathan Associates, Inc.

ALFRED C. NEAL, President
Committee for Economic Development

JOHN A. PERKINS
Graduate School of Management
Northwestern University

HOWARD C. PETERSEN, Chairman
The Fidelity Bank

3 C. WREDE PETERSMEYER
Chairman and President
Corinthian Broadcasting Corporation

PHILIP D. REED
New York, New York

MELVIN J. ROBERTS, Chairman
Colorado National Bank of Denver

WILLIAM M. ROTH
San Francisco, California

ROBERT B. SEMPLE, Chairman
BASF Wyandotte Corporation

1 S. ABBOT SMITH
Boston, Massachusetts

2 PHILIP SPORN
New York, New York

ALLAN SPROUL
Kentfield, California

WILLIAM C. STOLK, Chairman
W. C. Stolk & Associates, Inc.

ALEXANDER L. STOTT
Vice President and Comptroller
American Telephone & Telegraph Company

WAYNE E. THOMPSON
Senior Vice President
Dayton Hudson Corporation

H. C. TURNER, JR.
Chairman, Executive Committee
Turner Construction Company

HERMAN L. WEISS
Vice Chairman of the Board
General Electric Company

1 FRAZAR B. WILDE, Chairman Emeritus
Connecticut General Life Insurance Co.

WALTER W. WILSON, Partner
Morgan Stanley & Co.

THEODORE O. YNTEMA
Department of Economics
Oakland University

BUSINESS STRUCTURE AND PERFORMANCE SUBCOMMITTEE

Chairman

RAYMON H. MULFORD, Chairman
Owens-Illinois Inc.

1 WILLIAM H. ABBOTT
Director and Member of the
Executive Committee
3M Company

1 E. SHERMAN ADAMS
Senior Vice President and Economist
The Fidelity Bank

HAROLD BURROW, President
Burrow Enterprises

EDWARD W. CARTER, President
Broadway-Hale Stores, Inc.

1 WILLIAM S. EDGERLY
Financial Vice President
Cabot Corporation

WILLIAM H. FRANKLIN, President
Caterpillar Tractor Co.

2 REED O. HUNT
Crown Zellerbach Corporation

DAVID E. LILIENTHAL
President and Chairman
Development and Resources Corporation

1 FRANKLIN A. LINDSAY, President
Itek Corporation

JOHN F. MERRIAM
Chairman, Executive Committee
Northern Natural Gas Company

DeWITT J. PAUL
Beneficial Corporation

JAMES E. ROBISON
Chairman of the Board
Indian Head Inc.

DONALD B. SMILEY
Chairman of the Board
R. H. Macy & Co., Inc.

1 S. ABBOT SMITH
Boston, Massachusetts

1 SIDNEY J. WEINBERG, JR., Partner
Goldman, Sachs & Co.

THEODORE O. YNTEMA
Department of Economics
Oakland University

1. Voted to approve the policy statement but submitted memoranda of comment, reservation, or dissent, or wished to be associated with memoranda of others. See pages 62-74.
2. Voted to disapprove this statement.
3. Did not participate in the voting on this statement because of absence from the country.

5.

PROJECT DIRECTOR

CHARLES E. ALLEN
Charles Allen & Company, Inc.

ADVISORS TO THE SUBCOMMITTEE

ALFRED D. CHANDLER, JR.
Chairman, Department of History
The Johns Hopkins University

RICHARD M. CYERT
Dean, Graduate School of
Industrial Administration
Carnegie-Mellon University

RICHARD EELLS, Executive Editor
Studies of the Modern Corporation
Columbia Graduate School of Business

SOLOMON FABRICANT
National Bureau of Economic
Research, Inc.

RENSIS LIKERT
Chairman of the Board
Rensis Likert Associates

FRITZ MACHLUP
Director, International Finance Section
Princeton University

EDWARD S. MASON
Lamont University Professor
Harvard University

ALMARIN PHILLIPS
Professor of Economics and Law
Wharton School of Finance and Commerce
University of Pennsylvania

DONALD RAPPAPORT
Price Waterhouse & Co.

HANS B. THORELLI
Graduate School of Business
Indiana University

HENRY C. WALLICH
Department of Economics
Yale University

CED Staff Advisors
FRANK W. SCHIFF
HOWARD P. WHIDDEN

RESEARCH ADVISORY BOARD

Chairman
CHARLES L. SCHULTZE
The Brookings Institution

EDWARD C. BANFIELD
Department of Government
Harvard University

ALAN K. CAMPBELL
Dean, The Maxwell School of Citizenship
and Public Affairs
Syracuse University

WILBUR J. COHEN
Dean, School of Education
The University of Michigan

WALTER W. HELLER
Department of Economics
University of Minnesota

LAWRENCE C. HOWARD
Dean, Graduate School of Public
and International Affairs
University of Pittsburgh

CARL KAYSEN
Director, The Institute for Advanced Study
Princeton University

JOHN R. MEYER
President
National Bureau of Economic Research, Inc.

FREDERICK C. MOSHER
Woodrow Wilson Department of
Government and Foreign Affairs
University of Virginia

DON K. PRICE
Dean, John Fitzgerald Kennedy School
of Government
Harvard University

RAYMOND VERNON
Graduate School
of Business Administration
Harvard University

HENRY C. WALLICH
Department of Economics
Yale University

Associate Members
CHARLES P. KINDLEBERGER
Department of Economics and Social Science
Massachusetts Institute of Technology

MITCHELL SVIRIDOFF
Vice President, Division of National Affairs
The Ford Foundation

PAUL N. YLVISAKER
Professor, Public Affairs and
Urban Planning
Woodrow Wilson School of Public
and International Affairs
Princeton University

Foreword

_____

The steadily growing concern with the nation's social problems that has been demonstrated by business and other major American institutions during the past five years is reflected in the history of this policy statement. The study was undertaken early in 1966 by the Subcommittee on Business Structure and Performance under the chairmanship of David E. Lilienthal. As the subcommittee began its work, it expected to devote its main attention to defining the economic objectives which a satisfactory business structure might be expected to serve, and to recommend how performance in meeting these objectives might be evaluated. After 1967, however, the subcommittee gradually shifted its interest to the social problems which might be ameliorated by the efforts of business, especially large, professionally managed corporations. In the course of this change of emphasis Mr. Lilienthal went into government service and Raymon H. Mulford became chairman of the subcommittee.

The shift in the subcommittee's main interest came during a period in which CED was giving increasing attention to social problems and the importance of having both the public and private sectors make greater efforts to deal with these problems. Our concern showed up in the 25th Anniversary symposium of November 1967 on "Corporate Decisions for Social Progress." In summing up this symposium I had occasion to make the following points--that business should do much more to meet social needs, that we were not quite sure how to carry out this new business commitment to social problem-solving, and that to get results business and government would have to develop an effective partnership. For its part, the Research and Policy Committee during 1968 and 1969 authorized a series of policy statement studies in the social area, and the following policy statements were among those issued between February

1970 and March 1971: *Reshaping Government in Metropolitan Areas, Improving the Public Welfare System, Training and Jobs for the Urban Poor,* and *Education for the Urban Disadvantaged.*

The present policy statement, as well as those just mentioned, must be seen in the perspective of the growing consensus in our society that higher priority than ever before must be given to the nation's social problems. This statement also provides a perspective between two extreme views that have been argued for many years. At one extreme there has been the view—held much more strongly several years ago than it is today—that the main function of business is to produce maximum profits year by year. At the other extreme is the view that business, whether it was the source or not, has a major responsibility for resolving most of the social and environmental problems afflicting the nation. This statement charts a path between these extremes. Our goal in issuing it is twofold—to provide a useful guide to business enterprises in the difficult task of finding their appropriate role in helping meet the social problems faced by the nation; and, secondarily, to increase understanding by the public and government of the efforts business is making to meet this challenge in an effective way.

The short Introduction which follows this foreword explains why the Committee has addressed itself in this statement primarily to the *social* rather than *economic* aspects of business responsibility and why it has concentrated on large corporations. The Introduction also indicates why the questions of corporate structure and of the business-government interface, which are closely related to this statement, are not dealt with at any length but have been left for future studies.

I should like to extend the appreciation of the Research and Policy Committee to all the members of the subcommittee which prepared the statement, particularly to Chairman Raymon H. Mulford and his predecessor David E. Lilienthal, as well as to the subcommittee's advisors. Charles E. Allen, Project Director, deserves special recognition for the drafting of the statement, to which David C. Melnicoff and Harold F. Mayfield had contributed in earlier stages of the subcommittee's work.

Emilio G. Collado, *Co-Chairman*
Research and Policy Committee

8.

Introduction

This statement deals with the social responsibilities of business enterprises in contemporary American society. It is intended to contribute to a clearer view of these developing responsibilities and to show how business can best respond to the changing requirements of society.*

To focus sharply enough on such a complex and fluid situation, the Research and Policy Committee has defined its frame of reference in this way:

> • To address ourselves predominantly to the *social* rather than the *economic* aspects of business responsibilities, although we recognize that business serves society mainly through carrying out its basic functions of producing goods and services and generating wealth that improves the nation's standard of living.[1]

1/The economic performance of business has been treated in our earlier statement, *Economic Growth in the United States,* a Statement on National Policy by the Research and Policy Committee, Committee for Economic Development, updated and reissued by the Program Committee (New York: October 1969).

*See Memorandum by MR. PHILIP SPORN, page 62.

• To concentrate on the large publicly-owned, professionally-managed corporations which account for most of the country's productive capacity and which generally bear the burden of leadership within the business community. Nonetheless, much of what we say about social responsibilities applies as well to smaller enterprises and to businessmen as individuals.*

• To consider the structure of corporations as it affects social responsiveness and accountability, but not undertake a thorough analysis of organizational matters which would require a study in its own right.**

• Similarly, to treat business-government relationships as these impinge on our central concern with social responsibilities, without attempting a detailed analysis of the business-government interface which would also necessitate a separate study.

• Finally, we have restricted our scope to the United States to make the subject manageable, although we recognize that there are international implications and interactions involved in the social responsibilities and performance of American business enterprises operating abroad.

Within this frame of reference, we have sought to set forth a fresh and enlightened point of view about the role of business as an important instrument for social progress in our pluralistic society. While this statement emphasizes some general policies and new approaches which seem to us necessary to achieving better balanced economic and social development, it does not make specific recommendations for action as the Committee normally does in its statements on national policy. Primarily, this is an educational document which aims to provide the background and perspective for the development of solid reasoning and sound policy on the part of business, government, and the public.

---

*See Memorandum by MR. S. ABBOT SMITH, page 62.
**See Memorandum by MR. PHILIP SPORN, page 63.

1.
The
Changing
Social Contract
with
Business

Business functions by public consent, and its basic purpose is to serve constructively the needs of society—to the satisfaction of society.

Historically, business has discharged this obligation mainly by supplying the needs and wants of people for goods and services, by providing jobs and purchasing power, and by producing most of the wealth of the nation. This has been what American society required of business, and business on the whole has done its job remarkably well. Since 1890, the total real national product has risen at an average of more than three per cent a year compounded, almost doubling every 20 years. Even with a threefold growth in population and greatly increased taxes, real disposable income per person has more than tripled and work time has declined by a third over the past 80 years.

In generating such substantial economic growth, American business has provided increasing employment, rising wages and salaries, employee benefit plans, and expanding career opportunities for a labor force, many of whose members are still subject to intermittent unemployment, which has grown to 83 million people. More than 30 million stockholders—and some 100 million people who have life insurance policies, pensions and mutual fund shares—have benefited over many years from dividends and appreciation of their investments in business. All other major institutions of society, including government, have been sustained in substantial measure by the wealth produced by a business system which provides a strong economic foundation for the entire society.

Most important, the rising standard of living of the average American family has enabled more and more citizens to develop their lives as they wish with less and less constraint imposed on them by economic need. Thus, most Americans have been able to afford better health, food, clothing, shelter, and education than the citizens of any other nation have ever achieved on such a large scale.

Business has carried out its basic economic responsibilities to society so well largely because of the dynamic workings of the private enterprise system. The profit-and-loss discipline continually spurs businessmen to improve goods and services, to reduce costs, and to attract more customers. By earning profit through serving people better than their competitors, successful business concerns have been able to contribute importantly—through taxes and donations—to the financial support of public and private organizations working to improve the quality of life. By operating efficiently, business concerns have been able to provide people with both the means and the leisure to enjoy a better life.

Moreover, the competitive marketplace has served as an effective means of bringing about an efficient allocation of a major part of the country's resources to ever-changing public requirements.

Notwithstanding these accomplishments, the expectations of American society have now begun to rise at a faster pace than the nation's economic and social performance. Concentrated attention is being focused on the ill-being of sectors of the population and on ways to bring them up to the general well-being of most of the citizenry. Fundamental changes are also taking place in attitudes, with greater emphasis being put on human values—on individual worth and the qualitative aspects of life and community affairs.

Society has also become acutely conscious of environmental problems such as air and water pollution produced by rapid economic development and population pressures. And the public has become increasingly concerned about the malfunctioning of important community services such as those provided by the post office, mass transportation, and some utility systems; about inadequacies in education and health care; and about mounting social problems such as poverty, crime, and drugs.

There is now a pervasive feeling in the country that the social order somehow has gotten out of balance, and that greater affluence amid a deteriorating environment and community life does not make much sense.

The discontinuity between what we have accomplished as producers and consumers and what we want in the way of a good society has engendered strong social pressures to close the gap—to improve the way the over-all American system is working so that a better quality of life can be achieved for the entire citizenry within a well-functioning community. The goals include:

- elimination of poverty and provision of good health care

- equal opportunity for each person to realize his or her full potential regardless of race, sex, or creed

- education and training for a fully productive and rewarding participation in modern society

- ample jobs and career opportunities in all parts of society

- livable communities with decent housing, safe streets, a clean and pleasant environment, efficient transportation, good cultural and educational opportunities, and a prevailing mood of civility among people

These goals for some years have been articulated, advocated, and worked for by leaders in American politics, business, labor, and education. Their efforts have produced considerable progress toward most of the goals, and have contributed to the development of a broad consensus in support of more intensive efforts to realize all of them more fully, especially since the productivity of the economic system now makes this feasible.

Today there are also newer forces at work—pressing for rapid and, in some instances, radical changes in the social order. These include a highly idealistic and restless generation of American youth;

a cultural leadership class of writers, filmmakers, artists, and intellectuals which is exerting considerable influence through communications media, literature, theaters, and universities; and numerous citizens' groups which are crusading for conservation, consumerism, black power, and other objectives. Many of these movements tend to assault the status quo and "establishment" institutions, which are viewed as obstacles to social progress and as too rigidly orthodox.

More broadly, the sluggishness of social progress is engendering rising criticism of *all* major institutions—government, schools, organized labor, the military, the church, as well as business. In this context, the large business corporation is undergoing the most searching public scrutiny since the 1930's about its role in American society. There is widespread complaint that corporations have become cavalier about consumer interests, have been largely indifferent to social deterioration around them, and are dangerous polluters of the environment.

The interaction between protagonists of substantial reform of major institutions and a generally concerned citizenry is producing significant changes in public expectations of business. As evidence of this, studies by Opinion Research Corporation during 1970 show that:

> • Sixty per cent of the population 18 years and older still consider that a main responsibility of business is to satisfy consumer needs for more and better goods and services. Corporations get good marks for innovativeness in developing new products to improve the nation's living standards. But twice as many people think companies are not doing as much as they should to satisfy consumer needs at reasonable prices as those who believe business is doing a particularly good job for consumers. At the heart of this dissatisfaction is the complaint that consumers are not provided with sufficient product information to make wise choices, and sometimes are misled by deceptive packaging and marketing practices.

> • Most significant, 60 per cent of the electorate also consider that another main responsibility of business is to keep the environment clean and free of pollution. Public criticism has increased to the point where 49 per cent do not believe corporations are doing as much as they should to improve the environ-

14.

ment, as against only 7 per cent who think they are doing a particularly good job. Most of the public are not convinced that companies are making any real progress toward solving their pollution problems, and about 80 per cent favor closing plants that violate pollution regulations.

● Substantial percentages of the public also identify as main corporate responsibilities such functions as hiring and training blacks and other disadvantaged people (38 per cent); contributing money to support public education, health, and charities (36 per cent); and helping to clean up and rebuild the ghettos in big cities (29 per cent). Slightly more of the public is satisfied with corporate performance in philanthropic activities than those who believe companies should increase their contributions.

Over all, a clear majority of the public thinks corporations have not been sufficiently concerned about the problems facing our society. Two-thirds believe business now has a moral obligation to help other major institutions to achieve social progress, even at the expense of profitability.

The fact is that the public wants business to contribute a good deal more to achieving the goals of a good society. Its expectations of business have broadened into what may be described as three concentric circles of responsibilities.

The *inner circle* includes the clear-cut basic responsibilities for the efficient execution of the economic function—products, jobs, and economic growth.

The *intermediate circle* encompasses responsibility to exercise this economic function with a sensitive awareness of changing social values and priorities: for example, with respect to environmental conservation; hiring and relations with employees; and more rigorous expectations of customers for information, fair treatment, and protection from injury.

The *outer circle* outlines newly emerging and still amorphous responsibilities that business should assume to become more broadly involved in actively improving the social environment. Society is beginning to turn to corporations for help with major social problems such as poverty and urban blight. This is not so much because the public considers business singularly responsible for creating these problems but

15.

because it feels large corporations possess considerable resources and skills that could make a critical difference in solving these problems. Indeed, out of a mixture of public frustration and respect for the perceived efficiency of business organizations, there is a clear tendency to look to corporations to take up the slack resulting from inadequate performance of other institutions, notably government but also education and health care in some measure. At the same time, the weight of informed opinion seems to be that these tertiary areas are not the responsibility of business in the first instance but that of the public sector and/or other private institutions. Even so, there is growing support for a more self-conscious partnership between business, government, and other institutions in some of these areas, most of all in urban affairs.

These broadened expectations of business have been building up for some time. This is indicated by the trends in public opinion over a number of years, and by the resultant actions of government in responding to the public will through an increasing variety of measures to protect consumer interests, to clean up the environment, and to enhance equal opportunities for employment and career development in industry. The evidence strongly suggests that these are solid and durable trends, not momentary frustrations or fads, and that they are likely to increase rather than diminish in the future.

Public opinion trends, of course, are not the only criteria for formulating sound business or public policy. Yet public opinion is a basic consideration, and in democratic society it usually is determinative over the long run, as demonstrated throughout the history of American business.

Today it is clear that the terms of the contract between society and business are, in fact, changing in substantial and important ways. Business is being asked to assume broader responsibilities to society than ever before and to serve a wider range of human values. Business enterprises, in effect, are being asked to contribute more to the quality of American life than just supplying quantities of goods and services. Inasmuch as business exists to serve society, its future will depend on the quality of management's response to the changing expectations of the public.*

---

*See Memoranda by MR. PHILIP SPORN, and by MR. SIDNEY J. WEINBERG, JR., pages 63 and 64.

16.

2.
The
Evolving
Corporate Institution
and
Managerial
Outlook

The American business corporation, like the society in which it has its being, is a dynamic and changing institution. The corporation has gone through several major transformations and demonstrated great adaptability to societal changes over the past century. Its remarkable growth as an institution provides evidence of this fact. To survive, expand, and prosper it has had to adapt and serve society well.

Corporations have developed beyond anything imagined by the early economists. In Adam Smith's day and in his mind, the typical business establishment was that of the small entrepreneur who produced a simple product or service in competition with a large number of similar entrepreneurs.

American industrial enterprises on the modern scale had their beginnings in the middle of the nineteenth century with the spread of the railroad network and the steam-powered factory system. By the end of the century, many companies that had begun as comparatively simple organizations devoted solely to manufacturing had expanded to become vertical complexes embracing also the sources of raw materials and the marketing of products.

Corporate Growth and Responsibilities

During the twentieth century, corporations have grown enormously in size and power as they have followed the economic logic of complete integration from raw materials through all phases of manufacturing to the sale of products to the ultimate consumer. Many have also diversified horizontally into related and sometimes distinctively different lines of business, directed from a central management point. And a great many American corporations have also expanded internationally to such an extent that they have become truly global enterprises. They find raw materials wherever these are least costly, process them wherever it is most economical, transport goods great distances, and sell in the most advantageous markets irrespective of national boundaries.

Whether its size is dictated by the need for capital, mass production and mass marketing, or other forces, the large corporation has assumed a crucial role in the modern economy. The 500 largest American industrial corporations now account for nearly two-thirds of all domestic industrial sales, and 120 of these have annual sales exceeding $1 billion.

There have also been some notable failures as the profit-and-loss discipline weeded out enterprises which had become so poorly managed that they went into bankruptcy and were reorganized, or had ceased to be socially viable as independent firms and were absorbed into more efficient enterprises.

Contrary to fears of an earlier era, the growth of large corporations has not restricted opportunities for small enterprises to start up and flourish. Over the past 15 years, the number of proprietorships in the United States, comprising individually-owned businesses and farms, has increased from about 8 to 9 million, while active corporations have increased from about three-quarters to one and one-half million.

Nonetheless, the large corporations are the dominant producers in the industries in which they operate, and their influence is pervasive throughout the business world and much of society. Large corporations' price and wage changes strongly influence the economic actions of other companies—inside and outside their own industries. The leadership or inaction of large companies and their representatives frequently sets the pattern for the social performance of most of the business community—in terms of contributions to educational and cultural organizations, participation in job training and equal employment programs, and improvement of the environment.

As corporations have grown, they also have developed sizable constituencies of people whose interests and welfare are inexorably linked with the company and whose support is vital to its success. The constituencies include:

Employees—many major corporations have more than 100,000 employees, while some (G.M. and A.T.&T.) have about one million. Employees are usually dependent on the corporation for their livelihood, work satisfaction and career development, and often for much of their social life. Conversely, many employees wield considerable power within business organizations through their individual skills and through their labor unions, and increasingly exert important influence in community affairs.

Stockholders—many corporations have hundreds of thousands of stockholders who are dependent on the company in varying degrees for their income. The understanding and allegiance of these stockholders is very important because by buying in or selling out they affect the financial standing of the company in the market, its ability to raise capital and acquire other firms, and its general reputation.

Customers and consumers—most corporations also have millions of customers and ultimate consumers who look to the corporation for the products and services they want. Customers usually are not dependent on a single source and their allegiance must continually be courted. At the same time, the corporation can affect their purchasing habits through advertising and merchandising.

Suppliers—a major corporation has thousands of suppliers of all sizes who, in substantial measure, are dependent upon it as an important market. The purchasing company, in turn, looks to its suppliers not only for quality products and services at competitive prices but often as a source of technological innovation.

19.

Community neighbors—large corporations have operations in numerous communities throughout most of the country. Many of these operations are on a large enough scale in nonmetropolitan communities that they have considerable effect on the hundreds of thousands of people who live in or near such corporate facilities as mines, oil fields, forests, manufacturing plants, and research laboratories. The very appearance and tone of a small- or medium-size community, as well as its economic well-being, is often greatly influenced by its dominant industry. This is also true of cities as large as Seattle or Rochester.* In this symbiotic relationship, the goodwill of the community is a positive contribution to the morale and performance of the corporation and its employees as well as a factor in the corporate image nationally.

In fact, the constituencies of large corporations have become so sizable and diversified—encompassing millions of employees, stockholders, customers, and community neighbors in all sections of the country and in all classes of society—that they actually constitute a microcosm of the entire society.

Beyond its interrelationships with these constituencies, the corporation also continuously interacts with other important elements in our pluralistic society. There are the *competitors,* both the producers of the same type of product and others seeking to substitute new products, vigorously striving to take away customers. There are *labor unions,* sometimes competing with management for the allegiance, welfare, and wages of employees, sometimes cooperating in the pursuit of productivity and other common goals, and generally exercising strong political influence. There are a wide variety of *interest groups,* continually monitoring what the corporation does in conservation, employment, and other sensitive areas, and often agitating for specific changes in corporate behavior. There is *education* which has brought new kinds of business talent into the corporation, fostering ideas and pressures for change. There is the *press* and other media, alert to the news value of David and Goliath confrontations and to its watchdog role of publicizing any shortcoming of corporate as well as governmental institutions. There is *government* at federal, state, and local levels in its various capacities as customer, scrutineer, regulator, and lawmaker; and, in all instances, tax collector.

---

*See Memorandum by MR. GEORGE C. McGHEE, page 64.

In relations with their constituencies and with the larger society, American corporations operate today in an intricate matrix of obligations and responsibilities that far exceed in scope and complexity those of most other institutions and are analogous in many respects to government itself. *The great growth of corporations in size, market power, and impact on society has naturally brought with it a commensurate growth in responsibilities; in a democratic society, power sooner or later begets equivalent accountability.*

The growth of corporate responsibilities has been reflected in part by the growth of formal and informal constraints on the exercise of corporate power. A considerable body of law and government regulation has been developed to ensure that *all* corporations conduct business ethically, compete vigorously, treat employees fairly, advertise honestly, and so on. Corporations are also expected to behave in accordance with social customs, high moral standards, and humane values. Not all corporations have lived up to these standards, and increasingly the public reacts very strongly against those in positions of great power who are arrogant or insensitive to either their legal or social responsibilities.*

The New Managerial Outlook

As corporations have grown in ways that are visible from the outside, they have also been developing internally in ways which are not so obvious but are of great importance in shaping their role in society. The internal developments can be described in terms of the professional managers who have risen to the top in publicly-owned corporations. These new managers have brought about significant and continuing changes in corporate philosophy, organization, operations, and performance.

One of the most important changes is that the corporation is regarded and operated as a *permanent institution* in society. Whereas the proprietor of an earlier era saw his company as an expression of himself during his own lifetime and perhaps that of his sons, the professional manager sees the corporation as an institution very much more enduring than himself, an institution in which he plays a significant but transient role. In ascending to authority in a going enterprise, his aim is to

---

*See Memorandum by MR. FRAZAR B. WILDE, page 64.

21.

further the continuous institutional development of the corporation in a very long time frame. His obligation, therefore, is as much to plan for the future—for example, by investing substantially in long-range research or in planting trees which will be harvested in 60 to 80 years—as it is to improve the current operations of the company during what is usually a comparatively brief term of office.* His obligation is also to improve the qualitative aspects of the institution through the development of its personnel, the excellence of its performance, and its growing stature and reputation.

As a permanent institution, the large corporation is developing long-term goals such as survival, growth, and increasing respect and acceptance by the public.* Current profitability, once regarded as the dominant if not exclusive objective, is now often seen more as a vital means and powerful motivating force for achieving broader ends, rather than as an end in itself. Thus, modern managers are prepared to trade off short-run profits to achieve qualitative improvements in the institution which can be expected to contribute to the long-run profitable growth of the corporation.**

The modern professional manager also regards himself, not as an owner disposing of personal property as he sees fit, but as a trustee balancing the interests of many diverse participants and constituents in the enterprise, whose interests sometimes conflict with those of others. The chief executive of a large corporation has the problem of reconciling the demands of employees for more wages and improved benefit plans, customers for lower prices and greater values, vendors for higher prices, government for more taxes, stockholders for higher dividends and greater capital appreciation—all within a framework that will be constructive and acceptable to society.***

This interest-balancing involves much the same kind of political leadership and skill as is required in top government posts. The chief executive of a major corporation must exercise statesmanship in developing with the rest of the management group the objectives, strategies, and policies of the corporate enterprise. In implementing these, he must also obtain the "consent of the governed" or at least enough cooperation to make the policies work. And in the long run the principal constitu-

---

*See Memorandum by MR. MARVIN BOWER, page 65.
**See Memoranda by MR. MARVIN BOWER and by MR. WILLIAM S. EDGERLY, page 65.
***See Memorandum by MR. PHILIP SPORN, page 65.

encies will pass judgment on the quality of leadership he is providing to the corporate enterprise.*

Thus, recent generations of professional managers have been opening up more and more channels of communication and participation for various corporate constituences. Whereas the traditional management structure was almost exclusively concerned with raw materials, manufacturing, sales, and finance, the modern management group includes executives who give specialized attention to all the constituencies: employees, stockholders, suppliers, customers, communities, government, the press, and various interest groups.

Some new managers are concerning themselves with the role of the individual in large, highly-structured organizations. They are experimenting with new ways of restoring more of the sense of personality and craftsmanship that has been virtually extinguished in assembly-line operations. And, in some instances, encouraging progress is being made in enriching the jobs of blue-collar workers, fostering a spirit of teamwork, and bringing employees into fuller and more constructive participation in the corporate enterprise.

Increasing attention is also being given to broadening the composition and enhancing the effectiveness of boards of directors. In some instances, boards have been filled with cronies of the management who rubber-stamped its decisions. The trend today is toward more independent directors who take their fiduciary responsibilities seriously, bring expertise and insights from different fields to bear on management, and guide and audit the performance of the management group to optimize the development of the company as a whole.**

These developments in the organizational aspects of the corporation are of major importance and deserve deeper analysis and greater attention than can be given them in this statement. There is obviously under way a quest for better ways of integrating the various interests of major constituencies into the governance structure and processes and of relating the entire enterprise to society. In a broad sense, therefore, these developments are designed to make the corporation more responsive to its constituencies and to the larger society—while maintaining the managerial decisiveness that is required for efficient operations in the

*See Memorandum by MR. MARVIN BOWER, page 66.
**See Memorandum by MR. MARVIN BOWER, page 66.

23.

business world. Thus, the modern manager sees the corporation as a social as well as an economic organization, functioning in the whole of society rather just in the marketplace.*

All these developments are being greatly influenced by education. It is most significant that today's corporate leaders are the first truly college-educated generation of business executives. A *Fortune* survey of the chief executives of the 500 largest industrial corporations in 1970 showed that some 44 per cent had postgraduate degrees, another 36 per cent had undergraduate degrees, 14 per cent had some college education, and only 4 per cent had not attended college. The college education of these executives was almost equally divided among science and engineering, humanities and social sciences, and business administration. And their graduate degrees are equally diversified; about a third in business administration, and another third in law.

The full impact of education is just beginning to be felt throughout the managerial structure. Universities have been sending more than 20,000 MBA's alone into corporations each year. And several hundred thousand management people already in corporations are receiving additional formal management training each year.

Modern professional managers have been exposed to concepts of business and its relations with society that were not available to previous generations. Today's managers are also more involved in the world outside their business establishments through contact with people in many other sectors of society and through participation in public causes. They have a far better perception than their predecessors could possibly have had about society's problems, how the company looks from the outside, and how it impacts on society.

With the benefits of education and exposure, the modern manager is able to see the life of the corporation in terms of both its social and its economic ecology. A company functioning in the midst of a dynamic society may be compared to a living organism striving to live and develop within its environment. Relationships are extremely complex. The world around is at once sustaining and threatening. Multiple causes and multiple effects are continually at work. To be insensitive, even to subtleties, could be disastrous. It becomes necessary for the corporation's own existence that it be highly responsive to the environment in which it lives.**

---

*See Memorandum by MR. JOSEPH L. BLOCK, page 66.
**See Memorandum by MR. PHILIP SPORN, page 67.

3.
Enlightened Self-Interest: The Corporation's Stake in a Good Society

The changes under way in the corporate institution and managerial outlook are significant. They are tending to bring about a constructive response to growing public insistence that business take on more social responsibilities while continuing to improve the performance of its basic economic functions. *This process of adaptation of business structure and performance to the changing requirements of society can be facilitated greatly by the development of a clearer corporate rationale of the role business must play in the national community—a role as a responsible participant determined to resolve any conflict with humane values or the social environment.**

The development of this rationale needs to deal with such questions as:

• Why should corporations become substantially involved in the improvement of the social environment?

---

*See Memorandum by MR. ROBERT R. NATHAN, page 68.

- How can they justify this to their stockholders?
- How can companies reconcile substantial expenditures for social purposes with profitability?
- What are the limitations on corporate social responsibilities?

Some executives and economists argue that the business of business is just business; that management has no right and no qualifications to undertake activities to improve society, or to tax its constituents for such purposes, since the general welfare of society is a governmental responsibility. There are many who believe business should become more involved with public problems but who are nonetheless concerned that the assumption of broad social responsibilities could erode the professional discipline of profitability and blur the accepted criterion of corporate performance. *The answer to these quite legitimate concerns lies in a clearer perspective of business as a basic institution in American society with a vital stake in the general welfare as well as in its own public acceptance.*

The Doctrine of Enlightened Self-Interest

In classical economic thought, the fundamental drive of business to maximize profits was automatically regulated by the competitive marketplace. As Adam Smith put it, each individual left to pursue his own selfish interest (*laissez-faire*) would be guided "as by an unseen hand" to promote the public good.

The competitive marketplace remains the principal method of harmonizing business and public interests, because it has proved over a very long time to be an efficient way of allocating economic resources to society's needs. Yet governmental intervention has been required to promote and regulate the conditions of competition. Government also has intervened to guide economic activity toward major public objectives, as determined by the political process, when these cannot be achieved through the normal working of the marketplace.

The self-interest of the modern corporation and the way it is pursued have diverged a great deal from the classic *laissez-faire* model.

26.

There is broad recognition today that corporate self-interest is inexorably involved in the well-being of the society of which business is an integral part, and from which it draws the basic requirements needed for it to function at all—capital, labor, customers. There is increasing understanding that the corporation is dependent on the goodwill of society, which can sustain or impair its existence through public pressures on government. And it has become clear that the essential resources and goodwill of society are not naturally forthcoming to corporations whenever needed, but must be worked for and developed.

This body of understanding is the basis for the doctrine that it is in the "enlightened self-interest" of corporations to promote the public welfare in a positive way. The doctrine has gradually been developing in business and public policy over the past several decades to the point where it supports widespread corporate practices of a social nature, ranging from philanthropy to investments in attractive plants and other programs designed to improve the company's social environment.

In a 1935 amendment to the Internal Revenue Code, which for the first time permitted corporations to deduct up to 5 per cent of pretax income for charitable contributions, the doctrine was explicitly recognized by the state. Since then it has been substantially refined through corporate practice and sanctioned by the courts. *In various decisions, the courts have established the legality of corporate contributions for social purposes that serve the interests of the firm as broadly defined, even though they provide no direct benefits to it.* In the 1953 landmark A. P. Smith case, the New Jersey Superior Court upheld the right under common law of a manufacturing company to contribute funds to Princeton University. *The court held that it was not just a right but a duty of corporations to support higher education in the interest of the long-range well-being of their stockholders because the company could not hope to operate effectively in a society which is not functioning well.*

The basic reasoning is simply that a corporate grant, say to a department of engineering which will help to provide trained personnel for the company, is no less appropriate than a payment to a supplier of raw materials for inputs provided to the firm. Neither of these involves an intrusion of management into an area beyond its legitimate concern, and neither is in any sense a giveaway of the stockholders' resources.

By the same logic, expenditures to help improve community educational, health, and cultural facilities can be justified by the corpora-

27.

tion's interest in attracting the skilled people it needs who would not move into a substandard community. Similarly, a corporation whose operations must inevitably take place in urban areas may well be justified in investing in the rehabilitation of ghetto housing and contributing to the improvement of ghetto educational, recreational, and other facilities. In this case, of course, management must determine that these improvements are required to help make the company's environment safer and more acceptable to its employees and generally more conducive to effective business operations.

Indeed, the corporate interest broadly defined by management can support involvement in helping to solve virtually any social problem, because people who have a good environment, education, and opportunity make better employees, customers, and neighbors for business than those who are poor, ignorant, and oppressed.* It is obviously in the interest of business to enlarge its markets and to improve its work force by helping disadvantaged people to develop and employ their economic potential. Likewise, it is in the interest of business to help reduce the mounting costs of welfare, crime, disease, and waste of human potential —a good part of which business pays for.[1]

The doctrine of enlightened self-interest is also based on the proposition that if business does not accept a fair measure of responsibility for social improvement, the interests of the corporation may actually be jeopardized. Insensitivity to changing demands of society sooner or later results in public pressures for governmental intervention and regulation to require business to do what it was reluctant or unable to do voluntarily. Today, the public strongly wants the environment cleaned up and Congress is responding by enacting stringent anti-pollution measures which will require substantial technological and economic changes in many industries.**

_____

1/This is a moral proposition as well as a matter of self-interest. The corporation as a legal person has the same obligation as all citizens to participate in and contribute to the general welfare, and to treat human beings humanely. Many businessmen understand this and act from moral impulses—"we should do this because it's the right thing to do"—without explicitly calculating self-interest. They implicitly recognize that the corporation benefits from strengthening justice in the society. In civil rights, for instance, some businessmen acted on moral grounds in pioneering fair-employment practices long before this became legally required, in aiding black educational institutions, and in going well beyond the traditional scope of corporate activities to combat racial discrimination.

*See Memorandum by MR. MARVIN BOWER, page 69.
**See Memorandum by MR. ROBERT R. NATHAN, page 69.

28.

Public expectations are also expressed through direct citizen actions. In recent years, a number of companies have been challenged by racial, religious, and educational groups ready to divert purchases and investments away from firms not doing their part to eliminate barriers of discrimination in employment. Other companies have been confronted by petitions, by publicity generated by groups of indignant citizens, even by picket lines or more violent expressions of protest.

Experience with governmental and social constraints indicates that the corporation's self-interest is best served by a sensitivity to social concerns and a willingness, within competitive limits, to take needed action ahead of a confrontation. By acting on its own initiative, management preserves the flexibility needed to conduct the company's affairs in a constructive, efficient, and adaptive manner. And it avoids or minimizes the risk that governmental or social sanctions, produced out of a crisis atmosphere, may be more restrictive than necessary. Moreover, indiscriminate opposition to social change not only jeopardizes the interest of the single corporation, but also affects adversely the interest all corporations have in maintaining a climate conducive to the effective functioning of the entire business system.

Enlightened self-interest thus has both "carrot and stick" aspects. There is the positive appeal to the corporation's greater opportunities to grow and profit in a healthy, prosperous, and well-functioning society. And there is the negative threat of increasingly onerous compulsion and harassment if it does not do its part in helping create such a society.

Redefining Stockholder Interest

As a practical matter, the doctrine of "enlightened self-interest" applies to the stockholders of a corporation as well as to management and other participants in the enterprise. Yet some additional attention to this point is warranted because traditional economic theory holds that the stockholder's interest is served only by corporate investment policies which yield benefits that are fully recovered by the corporation, and therefore maximize the market value of its stock. Many corporate expenditures for social purposes—such as manpower training or urban renewal —produce benefits which cannot be fully recovered because the worker may move to another employer, or because environmental improvements also accrue to other businesses and to the public in general. Circumstances like these have tended to inhibit some corporations from expending funds for social improvements, especially when management doubts that such actions can be reconciled with what is presumed to be the "interest of the stockholder."

However, the widely diversified nature of business ownership today alters the interest of the stockholder as classically defined.[2] Nearly all investors now hold equities in more than one company. Moreover, a substantial and growing proportion of stockholder investment in business is not through individual portfolios of a few stocks, but through large investment media—such as pension trusts, mutual funds, and insurance companies—which invest regularly in hundreds of different companies in different industries. Stockholders' interests, therefore, tend to ride with corporations as a group and with investment policies which provide benefits to the corporate sector as a whole—in the form of improved environmental conditions, a better labor force, and stronger public approval of private business. That is, corporations as a group— and singly as well, under reasonable assumptions—will earn more on their invested capital, and stockholders will be better off if these broader investment policies are adopted.[*]

Inasmuch as the business community as a whole clearly has a vital stake in a good, well-functioning society, it can be argued that the stockholder's interest in the long run is best served by corporate policies which contribute to the development of the kind of society in which business can grow and prosper. Indeed, this long-range stockholder interest would justify governmental regulation to bring about improved environmental operating conditions—in, for example, pollution abatement—if corporations singly or as a group cannot achieve such results on their own.

Social Improvement and Profitability

The positive perspective of enlightened self-interest provides the

---

2/Henry C. Wallich and John J. McGowan, "Stockholder Interest and the Corporation's Role in Social Policy," in *A New Rationale for Corporate Social Policy,* CED Supplementary Paper Number 31 (New York: December 1970).

*See Memorandum by MR. WILLIAM H. ABBOTT, page 70.

framework for reconciling social improvement with profitability. Changing public expectations and the urgent quest for a good society are beginning to generate new demands for the kind of goods and services that in many respects business is demonstrably well qualified to provide. Some of these markets will come into existence fairly naturally, some will have to be created by business initiative, and others will have to be fashioned primarily by government. Altogether, they will provide substantial opportunities for business to profit by serving society's new requirements.

There are a great many social areas—such as housing, education, manpower training, health, transportation, large-scale urban redevelopment, and new cities—in which public pressures for improvement are already strong enough to create profitable markets, or markets that can be made profitable by a combination of greater business initiative and more effective governmental incentives. As these new opportunities develop, corporations with the entrepreneurial zeal to anticipate what the public is going to want, instead of merely supplying what it has wanted in the past, are apt to improve their profitability by discharging their responsibilities to society. Environmental quality standards, for instance, are creating large new markets for designers and producers of pollution-abatement equipment and systems, and for manufacturing process and technological changes that could eliminate industrial pollution at the source. Public pressures for social improvements, and the resultant market opportunities, will grow substantially over the next 30 years as the country has to provide for some 75 million more people and an even more highly urbanized population.

To respond to such opportunities, business must recognize that the pursuit of profit and the pursuit of social objectives can usually be made complementary. From the standpoint of business, profit can be earned by serving public needs for social improvements as well as for goods consumed privately. From the standpoint of society, public services can be improved by enlisting the efficiencies of business organizations through the opportunity for profit. Thus, market incentives can serve the common interest of business and society.

There are likely to be many areas of social improvement in which the prospects for profit do not meet prevailing corporate investment criteria. In such cases, corporations will need to reexamine the traditional concepts and measurements of profit in the newer context. This may well involve, among other things, a substantial diversion of resources away from private consumption into higher priority social improvements.*

Conversely, government will need to reexamine the comparative advantages of public- and private-sector capabilities for getting the great social tasks done as efficiently as possible. And government not only will have to develop an adequate pattern of incentives for business to do its part of the job in those social markets which otherwise would not be sufficiently attractive but also in some instances impose penalties on socially harmful activities.

Limitations
on Corporate Social Activities

Business establishments obviously cannot solve all the problems of society, with or without help from government. Corporations are necessarily limited by various internal constraints on what and how much they can do to improve society. One of the conditioning factors is corporate size and capability. A very large corporation with extensive resources and skills is able to do a good deal more than a small company which might have to stick exclusively to its traditional business to stay alive in a highly competitive market. Even the large corporation must give its main attention to its mainstream business to keep competitive, and it will have to find the best balance between these basic requirements and newer social market activities. Some companies may well find this balance on the social side because their interests, technologies, and skills are inclined in that direction. Others will not be well suited to do much more than extend their main lines of business into social markets wherever this is possible.

Cost-benefit considerations are a very important factor. No company of any size can willingly incur costs which would jeopardize its competitive position and threaten its survival. While companies may well be able to absorb modest costs or undertake some social activities on a break-even basis, any substantial expenditure must be justified in terms of the benefits, tangible and intangible, that are expected to be produced. Since major corporations have especially long planning hori-

*See Memorandum by MR. WILLIAM S. EDGERLY, page 70.

zons, they may be able to incur costs and forego profits in the short run for social improvements that are expected to enhance profits or improve the corporate environment in the long run. But the corporation that sacrifices too much in the way of earnings in the short run will soon find itself with no long run to worry about.

Thus, management must concern itself with realizing a level of profitability which its stockholders and the financial market consider to be reasonable under the circumstances. This means that substantial investments in social improvement will have to contribute to earnings, and the extent of such earnings will be a major factor in determining the mix of a company's commercial and social activities.

This suggests that criteria need to be developed for the range of profitability that will attract an adequate flow of corporate investment into various social markets. To be effective, the opportunities for profit should be reasonably related to comparable opportunities in traditional lines of business. In some cases, the risks might well be lower than in commercial areas, because competition is less or the social market is partially subsidized or guaranteed by government, and therefore the profit level can be correspondingly lower.

It can be expected that corporate social activities via the philanthropic route will be circumscribed by public policy considerations. Congress has established a ceiling of 5 per cent of pretax income on deductible corporate contributions. This is not currently restrictive because the average level of such contributions is only about one-fifth the allowable maximum, but it is a clear delineation of the scope of such activities.*

Corporate philanthropy is also constrained in many cases by management's reluctance in making grants to substitute its own judgment for the judgment of its various constituencies in society. Corporate philanthropy necessarily reflects the value system of management. The political process, in an imprecise but effective way, reflects the values of all constituencies. In such instances, management may prefer that the decisions be left to the political process in which all corporate constituents participate as well as management executives in their capacity as citizens. Exceedingly good managerial judgment will be required to achieve the right balance between the internal constraints on corporate leadership and external social needs and pressures.

---

*See Memorandum by MR. GEORGE C. McGHEE, page 70.

Clearly an alternative to philanthropy for supporting a social activity that is not only of particular interest to management but also of wide public benefit would be a new government program financed by taxation. Corporate participation in financing such programs through the corporate income tax amounts, at the marginal rate, to 48 per cent of profits. The history of corporate philanthropy contains many cases in which a social need was first met by philanthropy and later assumed by government.

In helping to meet social needs, as for better education or equal housing opportunity, companies may take the philanthropic route or lend support to government programs, or both. In addition, some may enter the business of providing the services needed on a profit-making basis. Thus, corporate activities in the social area encompass the full range from philanthropy through tax-supported government programs to profit-making business.

4.

Widening Parameters of Social Performance

As corporations recognize that their enlightened self-interest necessitates more substantial efforts to help improve their social environment, they are increasingly exploring and experimenting in new terrain. This reaching out into new social fields is in an embryonic stage, however. There is not sufficient accumulated experience to formulate the kind of strategy and methodology that is generally employed in the mainstream of corporate business.

Even so, there are patterns of corporate social involvement and performance that are beginning to emerge. These patterns, along with developments in business thinking and in social science research, can facilitate the formulation of needed guidelines and principles with respect to such questions as:

- What is the appropriate scope of corporate social involvement from the standpoint of management—considering the limitation of company resources, cost-benefit ratios, and good judgment about balancing the primary needs of the business with efforts to help improve social conditions?

● What is the appropriate scope from the standpoint of society— as judged by the comparative advantages in getting social problems dealt with by business corporations and by such other institutions as government, education, labor, private foundations, and volunteer groups?

● How much of the task can corporations undertake on an essentially voluntary basis under prevailing market conditions, and how much will need to be facilitated by changes in the governmental rules that govern the economic system?

● How can the social performance of business be evaluated?

Clarification of these issues would help society understand what business can reasonably be expected to accomplish, and how it can best be done. This could forestall exaggerated public expectations that corporations somehow can and should solve most of the country's social problems, and thus prevent a backlash of resentment when business performance falls short of unrealistic expectations. Conversely, clarification would facilitate the process by which business could find its optimum social role in a rational fashion. This would minimize the dual danger of under-response and resulting public dissatisfaction, or of over-response which could lead companies well beyond their competence, bring about destructive rivalry rather than healthy competition with other institutions, and stretch corporate capabilities so far as to sap performance in the mainstream business.*

Spectrum of Current Corporate Activities

The spectrum of aggregate business activities to improve society covers, in widely varying degrees, ten major fields. The following is a reasonably comprehensive list of the sorts of things being done by business in the aggregate; each company must select those activities which it can pursue most effectively.

---

*See Memorandum by MR. RICHARD C. GERSTENBERG, page 70.

Economic Growth and Efficiency

- *increasing productivity in the private sector of the economy*
- *improving the innovativeness and performance of business management*
- *enhancing competition*
- *cooperating with the government in developing more effective measures to control inflation and achieve high levels of employment*
- *supporting fiscal and monetary policies for steady economic growth*
- *helping with the post-Vietnam conversion of the economy*

Education

- *direct financial aid to schools, including scholarships, grants, and tuition refunds*
- *support for increases in school budgets*
- *donation of equipment and skilled personnel*
- *assistance in curriculum development*
- *aid in counseling and remedial education*
- *establishment of new schools, running schools and school systems*
- *assistance in the management and financing of colleges*

Employment and Training

- *active recruitment of the disadvantaged*
- *special functional training, remedial education, and counseling*
- *provision of day-care centers for children of working mothers*
- *improvement of work/career opportunities*
- *retraining of workers affected by automation or other causes of joblessness*

(continued)

- *establishment of company programs to remove the hazards of old age and sickness*
- *supporting where needed and appropriate the extension of government accident, unemployment, health and retirement systems*

Civil Rights and Equal Opportunity

- *ensuring employment and advancement opportunities for minorities*
- *facilitating equality of results by continued training and other special programs*
- *supporting and aiding the improvement of black educational facilities, and special programs for blacks and other minorities in integrated institutions*
- *encouraging adoption of open-housing ordinances*
- *building plants and sales offices in the ghettos*
- *providing financing and managerial assistance to minority enterprises, and participating with minorities in joint ventures*

Urban Renewal and Development

- *leadership and financial support for city and regional planning and development*
- *building or improving low-income housing*
- *building shopping centers, new communities, new cities*
- *improving transportation systems*

Pollution Abatement

- *installation of modern equipment*
- *engineering new facilities for minimum environmental effects*
- *research and technological development*

(continued)

38.

- *cooperating with municipalities in joint treatment facilities*
- *cooperating with local, state, regional and federal agencies in developing improved systems of environmental management*
- *developing more effective programs for recycling and reusing disposable materials*

Conservation and Recreation

- *augmenting the supply of replenishable resources, such as trees, with more productive species*
- *preserving animal life and the ecology of forests and comparable areas*
- *providing recreational and aesthetic facilities for public use*
- *restoring aesthetically depleted properties such as strip mines*
- *improving the yield of scarce materials and recycling to conserve the supply*

Culture and the Arts

- *direct financial support to art institutions and the performing arts*
- *development of indirect support as a business expense through gifts in kind, sponsoring artistic talent, and advertising*
- *participation on boards to give advice on legal, labor, and financial management problems*
- *helping secure government financial support for local or state arts councils and the National Endowment for the Arts*

Medical Care

- *helping plan community health activities*
- *designing and operating low-cost medical-care programs*
- *designing and running new hospitals, clinics, and extended-care facilities*

(continued)

  • *improving the administration and effectiveness of medical care*

  • *developing better systems for medical education, nurses' training*

  • *developing and supporting a better national system of health care*

Government

  • *helping improve management performance at all levels of government*

  • *supporting adequate compensation and development programs for government executives and employees*

  • *working for the modernization of the nation's governmental structure*

  • *facilitating the reorganization of government to improve its responsiveness and performance*

  • *advocating and supporting reforms in the election system and the legislative process*

  • *designing programs to enhance the effectiveness of the civil services*

  • *promoting reforms in the public welfare system, law enforcement, and other major governmental operations*

Corporate activities across this wide spectrum, notably in the areas of social progress, break down into two basic categories. First, there are purely voluntary activities where business takes the initiative and exercises leadership. Next are activities induced by government incentives, or required by law and regulations.

In this chapter, we examine those activities that are voluntary in nature—ranging from those which are generally considered as philanthropic to those which are essentially profit-making ventures in social markets.

40.

Voluntary Corporate Activities

Altogether, corporate contributions to "charitable and educational institutions" total nearly $1 billion a year. This represents a doubling of such contributions in slightly less than a decade, generally paralleling the rise in business profits and hovering around 1 per cent of total pretax corporate income.

A survey of patterns of giving in 1968 by 401 major corporations indicated that about 40 per cent of their contributions went to education; a slightly smaller proportion to united funds, hospitals, and organizations collecting for health and welfare; about 7 per cent to civic causes; about 5 per cent to cultural activities; and the remainder to miscellaneous groups. The emphasis has been shifting toward education, and in smaller but increasing amounts corporate grants are also flowing toward cultural and civic projects, such as symphonies, little theaters, libraries, and museums.

A number of corporations, especially larger ones, have taken steps in recent years to systematize and facilitate their philanthropic activities. Many have established contribution committees with secretariats specifically assigned to survey worthwhile projects, evaluate results of grants, and prepare annual contributions budgets. A large number, well over 1,500, have established company foundations to devote continuous and more professional attention to the philanthropic area, and to stabilize the flow of donations—e.g., during the economic downturn of 1969-71—by separating foundation resources from year-to-year fluctuations in corporate earnings.

A survey of more than 1,000 small, medium, and large corporations in 1967 showed that 92 per cent were making financial contributions to education, health, and welfare. The major corporations, which set the pace on most social fronts, actually lag behind smaller companies in philanthropy—averaging only about 0.66 per cent of their pretax income in 1968 as compared with 1 to 3 per cent for small concerns and the maximum allowable 5 per cent for several companies.

The greatest voluntary involvement of companies, of course, has always been in the *local community* where business support for social improvement programs is so traditional that it is generally taken for granted. Of more than 1,000 companies surveyed in 1967, 83 per cent reported that they made gifts of equipment and talent to community enterprises; 87 per cent said they encouraged employee participation in community service organizations, with most of them giving formal recognition for employees' public service; and 75 per cent also encouraged employee service on public boards and commissions.

Even in national problems such as racial discrimination, a company's concern usually is focused on the local community. This is true not only of smaller concerns, but also of major national corporations. As businessmen have come to realize the high costs and damaging effects of discrimination on nearly every aspect of society, many of them have directed the influence of their corporations not only to eliminating discrimination at the workplace but also in providing community leadership in solving this corrosive social problem.

Some companies have refused to build plants or offices in areas with restrictions on open housing until these were eliminated. As Robert D. Stuart, Jr., the president of Quaker Oats, put it:

> We expect to make a positive social contribution, as well as an economic contribution, wherever we go. Specifically in the area of race relations, we expect the communities we locate new facilities in to offer equal opportunities comparable to those we offer in our own employment.
>
> Thus, prior to our decision to locate a major food plant in Danville [Ill.] two and a half years ago—and of course Danville was interested in attracting new industry—we advised the city fathers that passage of an open-housing ordinance would impress us as an indication of the city's intent for social progress. The ordinance passed, and two days later we approved location of a new plant in Danville.[1]

Increasingly, voluntary corporate activities are also taking the form of *cooperative action*. Cooperation among firms has the advantages of pooling their talents, spreading the costs and risks of social improvement efforts, integrating these efforts and enhancing their effectiveness. These are a few examples:

- Under the auspices of Plans for Progress, some 37 clusters of companies have been formed to distribute help among predom-

---

1/ As stated in an editorial, "Something Socially Constructive," *American Banker* (October 9, 1970), p. 4.

inantly black colleges. Representatives of each cluster of seven or eight companies meet regularly at their "adopted" school and provide assistance in a multiplicity of ways: funds for specific projects, donation of equipment, consultation on technical problems, visiting lecturers, and summer positions for teachers.

• Two New York City corporations have established a profit-making venture, Construction for Progress, which is building about $6 million worth of low-rent apartment units in ghetto areas as turn-key projects. So far, construction has cost about 15 per cent less than it would have under governmental sponsorship, has been completed in one-third the time, and the first building has been sold to the New York City Housing Authority at a reasonable profit.

• On a larger scale, 30 leading companies in the Greater Hartford (Connecticut) region have established The Greater Hartford Corporation to plan and direct development of the 750 square-mile metropolitan area. As a profit-making operating organization, a development corporation is raising $30 million for the acquisition of land to produce a new community out of a North Hartford ghetto area as the first stage in a $3 billion regional development plan.[2]

• The life insurance industry has pooled its resources to provide some $2 billion in capital for long-term loans at low interest rates for redevelopment of ghetto areas.

Even so, the over-all pattern of voluntary individual and cooperative corporate activities to improve the social environment is quite spotty and not really substantial, either in terms of the magnitude of the nation's problems or of the business resources that could be applied to them. *These voluntary efforts need to be expanded and intensified. Voluntarism is a power that has always contributed a great deal to the improvement and functioning of our pluralistic, democratic society. It should be utilized to the fullest extent possible by the business commu-*

2/Hartford business leaders took this initiative not only because the cost of community services was rising rapidly but also because the quality of services was declining to the point that business would be most seriously affected unless a new and effective community life-support system were created.

43.

*nity in discharging its responsibilities to society. By exercising greater initiative and leadership, business can be more effective in shaping the future development of its social environment. In this way, business can guide change and enhance its operational scope and flexibility, rather than lapse into the constricting role of a rearguard defender of the status quo.**

Asserting the Initiative

Business enterprises have demonstrated many of the qualities and capabilities that appear to be critically needed in the solution of many of the country's social problems. They often possess comparative advantages over other institutions in such respects as innovation; technological competence; organizational, training and managerial abilities; and certain performance characteristics and disciplines. These comparative advantages could be more fully employed in relevant social areas, such as those in which corporate resources and experience can make a particular contribution or those with which the company has some logical connection.

Business itself could promote greater involvement in various ways. Top management, for example, could provide stronger leadership within many corporations to develop the policies and climate that would stimulate employees, especially young managers, to apply their interests and skills to relevant social as well as conventional business matters. The additional duty could be more widely and explicitly recognized as a normal, rather than extracurricular, part of managerial responsibilities, and as an essential ingredient for managers aiming to equip themselves for broader executive responsibility. Managers at all levels could be encouraged and given adequate incentives to seek out relevant social market opportunities for the corporation.**

The corporation itself can be organized for the systematic exploration and development of social markets *as a risk-taking, profit-making entrepreneurial line operation*. This requires not just the addition of staff specialists but also the development of new programs which are built into the main structure of the organization and its operating procedures. The restructuring might start by organizing a corporate "public

---

*See Memorandum by MR. E. SHERMAN ADAMS, page 71.
**See Memorandum by MR. GEORGE C. McGHEE, page 71.

44.

business" group under a top executive with adequate staff and funds. Such a group would research social market opportunities as vigorously as conventional markets, and would develop a strategic plan for capitalizing on these opportunities—the corporate resources that would be required, the priorities, the extent of company and of any intercompany involvement, the requirements if any for governmental incentives, and the results to be attained.

To mobilize the resources and skills required to deal with social matters that are too large and costly for any single company, major corporations might also exercise greater leadership in industry and trade associations, and in developing new consortium arrangements. So long as no restraint of trade is involved, these cooperative activities are permissible under the antitrust laws. If trade restraints may be involved, corporations should compete in social as well as any other markets unless in particular instances the public interest is clearly better served by specific governmental exemptions. In such cases, the government could permit the cooperative development under proper supervision of major new technological systems that are urgently required and cannot reasonably be produced by individual company efforts.

The possibilities of consortium arrangements should especially be explored on a more imaginative and vigorous basis. The consortium method enables corporations to form groups of companies which include all or most of the firms that would benefit from specific social improvements—such as improving educational, medical, and cultural facilities in their communities. In this way companies could recover the benefits completely or substantially enough to justify the group going ahead with a project which would not seem worthwhile to a single company or to only a few companies.

The consortium approach could also minimize competitive disadvantages, within reasonable antitrust constraints, of more substantial corporate expenditures or investments in larger-scale social improvements. In retrospect, corporations probably could and should have taken more initiative, individually and cooperatively, to abate industrial pollution prior to the onset of progressively more stringent governmental controls. Voluntary action on an equitable burden-sharing basis would have demonstrated business' willingness to accept and act on its social responsibilities to the fullest extent possible, would certainly have alleviated the problem, and would have defined more clearly the point at which regulation was not only necessary but desirable. *Indeed, if corporations cannot deal individually with major social responsibilities such as pollution because of competitive cost disadvantages, and if they are unable to cooperate in resolving such difficulties, then they logically and ethically should propose and support rational governmental regulation which will remove the short-run impediments from actions that are wise in the long run.* *

All this is to suggest that there is more scope for corporate initiative across the spectrum of philanthropic, burden-sharing, and profit-making social activities than has yet been realized. Even so, it is also clear that voluntary business actions alone will not be nearly sufficient to cope with the full range of corporate social responsibilities and to make the necessary contribution to the solution of the country's socio-economic problems. This will require government-business collaboration which is discussed in the next chapter.

Evaluation of Corporate Performance

As the corporation adapts to the changing requirements of society, and moves into uncharted social terrain, there is a clear need to develop better methods for determining corporate goals and evaluating performance.

At present, these goals are predominantly financial in nature. Performance is likewise measured in financial terms—earnings per share, return on investment, sales income. Yet as investors become more sophisticated, they are looking into other factors that are likely to influence the corporation's performance in the future—including its policies with respect to employment of minority groups, consumerism, and protection of the environment.

Security analysts, in particular, are probing deeply into management and are making judgments about the quality of the human organization and its capabilities for innovation and growth in changing environmental conditions. This is becoming an increasingly professional activity, and leading security analysts have much influence on the deci-

*See Memorandum by MR. THOMAS B. McCABE, page 72.

46.

sions of large investment groups to buy or sell a company's stock which, in turn, greatly affects its price in the market. Thus, the price-earnings ratio of a company's stock is made up of a *fact*—the measured and reported financial results—and a *judgment or opinion* about all the intangible and seldom reported factors that determine future performance. The importance of intangible corporate assets is also demonstrated by the substantial difference between a company's *book value* (which accounts only for the physical and financial assets) and its *market value* as established by the market price of its outstanding stock.

Until recently, these intangible assets could be appraised only by informed opinion and good judgment because there were no known ways to quantify them. However, a group of social scientists at the University of Michigan is developing theories and methodologies which could provide the means for measuring the worth of the productive capability of a firm's human organization, and may even eventually allow the value of the goodwill of its customers, stockholders and financiers to be more systematically taken into consideration.[3] They are also applying experimental systems of human asset accounting in business.

These efforts could in time provide managers with additional means of determining how to use the full resources of the business in the most productive and socially adaptive manner. The Michigan group, for example, has found that some of the conventional methods of cutting costs, increasing productivity and improving current earnings actually tend to have the opposite long-term effect by impairing the functioning of the human organization. The ability to detect and measure such changes in the human organization could enable management not only to improve its long-run economic performance but also to discharge better a responsibility to the key employee constituency which frequently influences community and public attitudes toward the company.

Improved measurement methods might also facilitate the governance of the corporate institution with respect to such other constituencies as investors and customers. In balancing the interests of various claimants, management needs to know as much as possible about the effects of products and of pricing and marketing practices on consumer satisfaction; the impact of a high wage settlement on stockholders; or

---

3/Rensis Likert, "The Influence of Social Research on Corporate Responsibility," in *A New Rationale for Corporate Social Policy*, CED Supplementary Paper Number 31 (New York: December 1970).

the employee reaction to increased executive compensation and dividends. Conversely, more objective and accurate information about the business could enable these and other constituent groups to play a more constructive role in helping optimize the results for *all* those who have a stake in the enterprise.

Most important, the development of improved social indicators and measurement techniques would aid management in finding the most appropriate corporate role in social improvement, determining the correct strategy, evaluating the results, and justifying its actions to its constituencies. At present, many businessmen and economists are hesitant about corporations moving into social activities because neither social requirements nor corporate capabilities, actions, and results can be quantified with the exactness of commercial activities. Correspondingly, corporate constituencies and the larger society lack adequate means for judging what the corporation is really accomplishing in efforts to improve its environment.

The mounting public demands for better social performance necessitate corporate goal setting and performance measurements—just as demands are being made for an improved process for formulating objectives and measuring performance in government.[4] There is little in the present accounting and reporting systems of corporations that enables anyone to determine whether corporations have well-formulated sets of goals for social performance, or to measure the extent of progress toward realization of these goals.

The first step is to formulate corporate goals, not just for the stockholder constituency in financial terms but also for all constituents in as definitive terms as possible, and for the relevant scope of corporate social activity. For example, it should be possible to establish reasonably tangible goals with respect to pollution abatement on the basis of air and water quality standards and criteria projected three to five years ahead. Similarly, goals with respect to employment and advancement of minorities can be projected without great difficulty.

The second step is to utilize the advanced methodologies which are beginning to emerge to develop means for measuring corporate performance in meeting its various goals. Some of this may not be as difficult as it seems. The biological oxygen demand (BOD) load of

---

4/This subject is being covered in a forthcoming CED Statement on National Policy, *Improving Federal Program Performance.*

effluent on receiving waters is now being measured precisely as are an increasing number of other pollutants, and these measurements can be related to goals previously determined.

The third step is to report to the corporate constituencies and the interested public the definitive measurements of performance toward established goals. These clear objective evaluations of actual corporate performance will be more credible to the public than general rhetoric about how well the company is living up to its social responsibilities; they will also be much more meaningful than expenditure data alone.*

By operating in a goldfish bowl of reporting progress toward goals, a management veering too far in pursuit of one constituency to satisfy its interest at the expense of another is likely to be brought into check by those whose interests are slighted. In the *laissez-faire* system, it was the *unseen hand* that was counted on to lead the pursuit of selfish private interests into realization of the public good. In the alternative system suggested here, it is the *visible hand* that is expected to achieve the same result.

---

*See Memorandum by MR. FRANKLIN A. LINDSAY, page 73.

5.

A
Government-Business
Partnership
for
Social
Progress

As business exerts greater initiative and ingenuity in exploring social fields, there is gradually evolving a new kind of partnership with federal, state, and local governments that holds great promise for the future. Governments, pressing against the limits of what can effectively be accomplished through public agencies, have been turning increasingly to business and other private organizations for help in carrying out public functions.

Beginning in the 1960's, the federal government encouraged business to perform an increasing variety of social tasks that had been regarded as almost exclusively governmental responsibilities, such as training disadvantaged persons, rebuilding the ghettos, helping blacks and other minorities establish their own enterprises. Inasmuch as business could not be expected to undertake many of these social tasks mostly at its own expense, government has sought to provide sufficient inducement to get the desired amount of business participation. Thus,

50.

E.T.S.U AT TEXARKANA

more liberal F.H.A. and veterans loans and rent supplements have been applied to create a better market for private construction of housing for low-income families. Contract subsidies are being used increasingly to induce corporations to employ and train disadvantaged people who normally would not have been considered qualified for jobs.

This tendency, sometimes called "privatizing" the public sector, reflects growing governmental and public acceptance of four important propositions:

- That the goals of American society can be realized only through a massive, cooperative effort of government, industry, labor, and education. Increasingly it is felt that the cooperative participation of the private sector is required not only for national defense and space exploration but also for advances in health care, improvement of education, and elimination of poverty.

- That government's basic role through the political process is to determine the nation's goals, set the priorities, develop the strategies, and create the conditions for carrying out the work most effectively to the satisfaction of the public.

- That business, with its profit-and-loss discipline, has an especially significant role in the actual execution of social programs because it is a proven instrument for getting much of society's work done and because its top executives, with their diverse management capabilities and their involvement in community affairs, are normally well fitted to deal with today's socioeconomic problems.

- That the incentive for profit is the only practicable way of unleashing the power and dynamism of private enterprise on a scale that will be effective in generating social progress. Social consciousness and good citizenship, while important prerequisites, cannot realistically be expected by themselves to bring business resources to bear on the country's social problems on the massive scale that is needed. To achieve this, government must create the market conditions that will induce business enterprises to apply their operational capabilities to those public tasks they can carry out more efficiently than other institutions.

51.

This clarification of the most suitable and effective roles for government and business—and, indeed, for other institutions such as education and labor*—is fundamental to the development of a viable national strategy for achieving the level of social progress that the public is demanding. It involves a substantial change in patterns of institutional responsibilities which have developed since the 1930's but are now clearly inadequate to the country's needs. Government at all levels seems likely to function best as a market creator, systems manager, and contractor of social tasks rather than as an actual operator of every kind of public service.

Governmental Incentives

The most desirable and effective form of governmental action to get business to contribute its dynamism to appropriate social areas is to create adequate markets in which private enterprise can compete as vigorously and efficiently as it does in consumer markets. This is the best way to bring the full force of market dynamics into play in the social and public service sector, and to achieve the drive for productivity and performance that is so conspicuously lacking in many of these sectors today. Moreover, the creation of competitive markets will minimize the risk of a social-industrial complex developing along lines of the so-called military-industrial complex.

The housing field offers a good example of some of the ways in which government can provide the additional incentives to create a market and induce the entrepreneurial thrust of business to achieve desirable social results. Eli Goldston, president of Eastern Gas and Fuel Associates, has described the effects of incentives in two large F.H.A. rehabilitation programs in a Boston ghetto:

> The principal incentive to private involvement in the first . . . program is rent supplements. The government assumes that a tenant can afford 25 per cent of his income for rent and makes up to the landlord the difference between this figure and the

*See Memorandum by MR. THOMAS B. McCABE, page 73.

"economic rent" that must be charged to return a reasonable profit under the F.H.A. formula.

In the second program, . . . the profit opportunity to the developer comes through F.H.A. mortgage loans at 3 to 3½ per cent, which lower the fixed charges of the projects. This makes possible quite low rentals and creates an attractive business opportunity in apartment rehabilitation. Here the tenants are expected to pay the full "economic rent," which, of course, is at a rate approved by the F.H.A.

[As a result,] the F.H.A. has enlisted private developers in the complete renovation of almost three thousand dwelling units within less than one calendar year . . . to bring . . . one of every seven Negro families in a rapidly declining city area out of deplorable substandard housing and into thoroughly modernized dwellings.[1]

Government could create major new markets not only in such areas as urban redevelopment and the building of new cities, but also in mass transportation, medical services, education, and many municipal services. The market-creation technique essentially is to bring about adequate demand conditions to attract competitive sources of supply. This can be done by pooling demand, when government, for example, assembles an entire land area required for urban renewal; or by enhancing purchasing capabilities, as in the case of subsidies to home buyers; or by providing credit and profit incentives to suppliers such as home builders.

The potential of competitive markets in municipal services is illustrated in a 1970 study by the New York City administrator's office. The study recommended that "the Department of Sanitation should gradually be reduced in size and scope and the private cartage industry be given the opportunity to expand . . . This would stem and even reverse the increase in taxes that have been spent to support an inefficient department." The New York study says that private cartmen can collect refuse at $18 a ton while paying taxes and making a profit, whereas the sanitation department's cost is $50 a ton. Similar New York City studies show correspondingly sharp increases in costs in many other municipal services with little or no increases in efficiency.

1/Eli Goldston, "New Prospects for American Business," *Daedalus* (Winter 1969), p. 97.

Government is beginning to search for more innovative and effective educational methods. In 1970, the Office of Economic Opportunity initiated a $6.5 million experimental program with six private business concerns. Entitled "performance contracting," its goal was to raise the reading and mathematics skills of some 28,000 disadvantaged students in 16 states. To receive any payment at all under the OEO performance contract, a participating firm must raise a child's achievement at least one full grade level. For this it will receive $110 per child. Since the firm provides all its own equipment and educational materials, to break even it must improve a student's ability by one and a half grades, or about three times the normal progress made by a disadvantaged child. The companies are using a variety of innovative techniques: teaching machines, revised curricula, incentive payments, and time off for students as well as teachers.

Also in 1970, the Banneker Elementary School in Gary, Indiana became the country's first public school to be operated by a private concern. Under a contract with the Gary board of education, Behavioral Research Laboratories of Palo Alto, California, has taken over the school, organized and staffed it, paid rent on the building, and provided all learning materials—for $800 per student, which is Gary's cost per pupil. At the end of three years, the firm will refund the fee paid for any of the 840 black students who have not been brought up to or above national grade level norms in all basic curriculum areas (about 75 per cent have been below such norms).

Hard-core unemployment is another social problem area where incentives were instituted in 1968 to attract business involvement after three decades of generally unsuccessful governmental efforts to train and find jobs for disadvantaged persons. The federal JOBS (Job Opportunities in the Business Sector) program, spearheaded by the National Alliance of Businessmen, provides for Department of Labor contracts with business enterprises to reimburse them for the special costs involved in the extensive education and training required by unemployed persons with little or no skill and experience. Through December 31, 1970 total hiring under the JOBS program had reached 610,000 of which about 30 per cent was accomplished under contract subsidy. Some 309,000 of these employees remained on their original jobs at the end of 1970, and many others left for more desirable jobs elsewhere.

Future Development of Incentives

The evidence clearly indicates that many of the goals of American society can best be realized by developing a system of incentives for private firms to do those social jobs which business can perform better and more economically than other institutions. Indeed, the entrepreneurial thrust of business—if encouraged, guided, and carefully audited by government at all levels—may well be indispensable in achieving a permanent solution to the urban and other socioeconomic problems that have badly overtaxed the capacity of public agencies.

A more extensive system of incentives should be developed quite carefully to ensure that the most appropriate measures are used to produce the desired action by business enterprise, that these are tailored precisely to each situation, and that the results are evaluated by competent agencies and accounted for to the public.

The most important specific incentives are:

Contracts

Government contracting for services and supplies in fiscal 1970 amounted to $48 billion or 25 per cent of federal government expenditures. Most contracting was for military procurement, space exploration, and research and development; and about 80 per cent of these contracts contained incentives for performance to achieve preset cost or price targets and include penalties for inadequate performance. There is also a considerable variety and an increasing amount of contracting-out of social tasks. The Social Security Administration, for example, contracts with the nonprofit Blue Cross Associations, profit-making insurance companies, and other enterprises to serve as agents for the federal government in receiving claims from and making payments to hospitals or doctors for services rendered to those covered by Medicare. The Veterans Administration contracts for the services of civilian hospitals and physicians for the dependents of military personnel in some circumstances, and it contracts with private insurance companies for the carrying of life insurance on veterans.

Cash subsidies

The federal government pays cash subsidies to a wide variety of recipients, ranging from farmers to certain commercial airlines.

As a form of subsidy, cash payments offer some obvious advantages in that their cost is easily determined and controlled. They are administered readily because the recipients are clearly identified and subject to loss of payments if they violate program requirements. Cash payments are also the only type of subsidy that is identified explicitly in the federal budget and is subject to the discipline of the appropriation process.

Loans, credit guarantees, insurance

Direct loans outstanding to the private sector at the close of fiscal 1970 amounted to some $51 billion in federal funds. Nearly $15 billion of this represented housing loans, and most of the rest was for export credit, agricultural credit and small business loans. Federal credit is extended primarily to meet those needs "affected with the public interest" which entail risk that limits the availability of private credit. A sizable part of the housing loans are made to finance the construction of housing in slum areas, where high economic and other risks discourage financing by private institutions, and interest rates are held deliberately below private credit charges. Similarly, credit guarantees, and mortgage and other insurance are designed to reduce risk, facilitate financing, and provide further incentive for business to undertake socially desirable activities.

Tax benefits*

Tax incentives in the form of timing advantages include such provisions as accelerated depreciation, current deductions for what might otherwise be capital items (as in the case of research and development expenditures), and soil and water conservation expenses. Other measures which provide incentives through differential tax treatment include such items as percentage depletion, capital gains, and the investment credit (now discontinued). The benefits of the resulting increase in investment and in economic activity tend to be widely dispersed.

On the other hand, where the focus on desirable social goals is much narrower, there may be some question as to the value of tax incentives. Under these conditions, it may be difficult to use tax incentives effectively because they cannot be applied specifically to individual com-

---

*See Memorandum by MR. ROBERT R. NATHAN, page 74.

pany and job requirements, administered with the degree of assurance required, or easily altered to meet changing conditions. Accordingly, where these considerations are important it may be preferable to utilize contractual incentives or direct subsidies to afford a greater degree of control as to application and results.

In developing a much more extensive system of economic incentives so that business can and will undertake more of the nation's social improvement tasks, two guiding principles will be of special importance:

1. Greater business involvement should be induced only in those areas of activity in which private enterprise is qualified to do a better job than other institutions. In areas such as education, professionals are certainly better qualified than businessmen to teach students. But business can and should be encouraged to contribute its managerial and organizational skills to strengthen the performance of educational and other institutions when necessary, although not in any sense to displace them.

2. The specific incentives provided to business should be primarily contractual in nature, or in the form of subsidies reflected in the expenditure side of the federal budget rather than in the form of special tax incentives. The budgetary process is the best means for allocating public funds among the full spectrum of competing public requirements, since the allocation is subject to legislative and public scrutiny and review. The process is increasingly being accompanied by performance evaluation to determine how well the intended objectives are met. Its integrity should be respected and it should be utilized to the fullest.

Governmental Controls and Disincentives

There is also a wide variety of governmental controls, regulations, and disincentives designed to influence the social performance of business. Government contractors, for example, have been forbidden to discriminate in hiring and in promoting blacks. This prohibition has been extended under the Civil Rights Act to all employers of 25 or more persons. Another example is the extensive body of regulation that has been developed in recent years to reduce air and water pollution from industrial and other sources.

These and other regulatory measures are essential in many fields to insure that *all* businesses, not only the financially strong and more socially responsible ones, act in accordance with the public interest. While business should develop its capacities for self-regulation and self-policing to the fullest extent possible, there are bound to be areas beyond the effective reach of these self-imposed constraints which can be regulated effectively only by government. This has proved to be the case with various automobile safety features, initiated by individual companies, which had to be prescribed as standard equipment through federal regulations. And it has also proved essential in pollution abatement where competitive pressures militated against an adequate response from all industry. The business world has in some cases responded better to environmental needs under a government system of general regulations that apply to all competitors, cover all sources of pollution including municipalities and agriculture, and distribute the cost burden equitably.

On the other hand, administrative regulations usually cannot deal neatly with the diseconomies involved in the environmental situation or with the complex trade-offs throughout the ecosystem.

The basic problem of environmental pollution is that clear air and pure water have long been used as free goods. Clean air and water have now become scarce commodities and should be treated as such. In economic terms, this means putting a price on their use, much as the market does with other scarce commodities such as labor and materials.

Administrative regulations have this effect by requiring expenditures for the abatement of pollution to the extent necessary to meet governmental standards. There is a possibility that a system of economic disincentives—such as fees or taxes on specific pollutants like lead or sulfur—might enable the market mechanism to bring about environmental improvements at lower cost than exclusive reliance on regulations. Such disincentives may also in some circumstances have effect more quickly than regulations, the enforcement of which frequently has been exceedingly cumbersome and slow. However, the economic situation may often be so complicated and imperfectly understood that time-consuming experimentation will be required to find precisely the right level of taxation to achieve desired results, and difficulties are entailed in adapting taxation to geographic differences in the need for control.

58.

New Forms
of Public-Private Enterprise

The converging of two trends—the business thrust into social fields, and government's increasing use of market incentives to induce even greater business involvement—is gradually bringing these two powerful institutions into a constructive partnership for accelerating social progress. This emerging partnership is more than a contractual relationship between a buyer and seller of services. Fundamentally, it offers a new means for developing the innate capabilities of a political democracy and a private enterprise economy into a new politico-economic system capable of managing social and technological change in the interest of a better social order. It by no means will be an exclusive partnership, for other private institutions, especially universities, will also play very significant roles. Still, the government-business relationship is likely to be the central one in the last third of the twentieth century.*

More effective means must be found to harness the technology, managerial capability, and efficiency of business in a large-scale organized manner to the capabilities of government and other institutions to operate effectively on major socioeconomic problems. These problems by their very nature require the best qualities and skills of both government and business plus, in some respects, the knowledge and research resources of universities.

New hybrid types of public-private corporations may need to be developed to combine the best attributes of government (funds, political capacity, public accountability) and of private enterprise (systems analysis, research and technology, managerial ability) in the optimum mix for dealing effectively with different kinds of major socioeconomic problems such as modernizing transportation, rebuilding the cities, and developing backward regions of the nation. Public-private corporations not only could provide the essential framework for blending government and business capabilities but also could contribute to the synergistic effect that seems to be needed to solve problems that so far have defied conventional attacks. Prototypes of these future public-private institutions already exist. They include such organizations as Comsat

---

*See Memorandum by MR. WILLIAM S. EDGERLY, page 74.

(Communications Satellite Corporation), Amtrak (National Railroad Passenger Corporation), and the National Corporation for Housing Partnerships.

More and different types of such institutions could be chartered as needed by appropriate governmental entities: a city, state, group of states in a region, or the federal government. The most important characteristic of these public-private corporations would be the best combination or mix of public and private resources to achieve designated objectives.

In general, government's involvement might include:

- A major share of responsibility for financing through appropriations, public borrowing, loan guarantees.
- Over-all planning so that the corporation's activities fit sensibly into the total environmental system in which it operates.
- Public accountability through a board of directors, partially elected and partially appointed, whose tenure (perhaps seven years) overlaps political terms to insulate the corporation from political pressures.

As for business involvement, it might include:

- Managerial and operating responsibilities, harnessing the entrepreneurial drive and managerial skills of the competitive business world.
- Research and development, in which business has great experience with the kinds of technological systems research and process/product development that are most needed in social improvement.
- Marketing, in terms of the public-private corporation's distribution of product and services to its customers and their continual adaptation to customer needs and tastes.

We welcome these developments. Management already is engaged in the process of change and revitalization of the corporate structure to improve economic and social performance and political accountability to its constituencies and society.

The need now is for new, innovative business relationships with government—federal, state, and local. Public expectations of more effective social action from both business and government are very great.

60.

We believe they call for renewed appraisal of the respective capabilities and roles of both institutions, and increased creativity in defining relationships between them.

Conclusion

We have sought in this statement to develop a clearer view of the business enterprise as an integral part of our pluralistic society, and as a full and responsible participant in the national community. We believe this is the perspective required to sustain and promote the essential economic functions of business, and to release the full productive and organizational capacities of the corporation for the benefit of society.

We have also attempted to open up a vista of business pioneering in new fields of activities, new societal responsibilities, and new cultural achievements that will be a new frontier for business over the next several decades. And we have suggested that responsible management must have the vision and exert the leadership to develop a broader social role for the corporation if business is to continue to receive public confidence and support. We have suggested as well that there are limitations to what business can contribute to social progress, and that the kind of society we want can be achieved only with the full participation of government and through major contributions from all our institutions —in education, medicine, religion, labor, the arts, philanthropy, and many other fields.

We believe business will respond constructively to this new challenge, as it has to many others in the past, and that it will contribute significantly to the common task of greatly improving the quality of life in the United States.

Memoranda
of Comment,
Reservation, or
Dissent

Page 9—By PHILIP SPORN, with which REED O. HUNT has asked to be associated:

I do not approve the statement for a number of reasons indicated here and in my subsequent comments.

The objective and drive of the report are given in the second sentence of its introductory statement: "It is intended to contribute to a clearer view of these developing responsibilities and to show how business can best respond to the changing requirements of society." I submit that what society requires from business has not changed significantly in recent years: If business is not meeting society's requirements it is not because they have changed but simply because business has not done a good enough job in its main area of responsibility. Thus this basic statement gives currency to a fallacy.

Page 10—By S. ABBOT SMITH:

It must be realized that this will be especially difficult for small businesses which are limited as to capital and personnel.

62.

Page 10—By PHILIP SPORN, with which REED O. HUNT has asked to be
associated:

What society wants from business is clearly indicated by examining a few typical cases. In the case of the railroad industry, for example, which is in deep trouble, what society wants and has not received
is an imaginative modern system of transportation supplying both passenger and freight service. For many years what the railroad industry
has been furnishing has not even approached that standard.

If the New York telephone communication system is in trouble
today, it is not due to changing conditions or requirements but primarily
because what had been for decades the best telephone service in the
world has over a period of recent years deteriorated badly to where it is
perhaps no better than third rate.

Once more, if many of the electric utilities of the country are in
trouble, it is not because of new requirements but because they have not
taken care of their basic responsibility to give an adequate power supply,
always reliable and not subject to sudden cataclysmic failures. That they
have also been careless of their obligations to do so with minimal adverse
effect on the environment has not helped them to get public absolution
of their failure to discharge their primary responsibility.

And if our automobile manufacturing industry is in difficulty, it is
due to the fact that for too many years the manufacturers and purveyors
of automobiles have, for competitive reasons, failed to realize that they
could not continue to build the same automobiles, making them larger
and more expensive, with more chrome plate and more horsepower under
the hood, while at the same time neglecting safety and the Frankenstein
of environmental pollution they were raising.

Page 16—By PHILIP SPORN, with which REED O. HUNT has asked to be
associated:

For the reasons indicated in my two comments above (pages 9
and 10), it seems to me that, before we in CED become too ambitious
and try to lay down a program covering a broad spectrum of more or less
desirable social activities by business, we would do better if we concentrated on a report on what business needs to do to more effectively discharge its responsibility qua business, each business in its respective
area. Such a report, prepared with proper concern for scholarship and
using as a perfectly solid guide the quotation of Alfred North Whitehead

63.

given on the inside front cover of the report, could be a great document for business, but its proper title then would be not "Social Responsibilities of Business Corporations" but "The Primary Responsibilities of Business." This report would also be consistent with the great philosophy of human activity promulgated more than two centuries ago by Voltaire, which is still as sound today as the day he uttered it: "Let us cultivate our garden." The fact that the report fails to do all this makes it impossible for me to accept it.

Page 16—By SIDNEY J. WEINBERG, JR.:

This report makes clear that large corporations have unique capabilities to aid in the accomplishment of important social goals. Further, the public's expectations of what business corporations can do in this regard are rising and are, in fact, properly encouraged in this report.

However I believe this should be emphasized—for corporations to participate meaningfully in reaching social goals, they must be profitable and the business economy must be productive and demonstrating "real" growth.

This means that to avoid developing misunderstandings and frustrations: (a) business cannot for long allow social involvement to dilute substantially economic-profit performance; (b) the public must realize that successful corporate involvement in these critical issues cannot be realized independently from a high-performance economy.

Page 20—By GEORGE C. McGHEE, with which CHARLES KELLER, JR. has asked to be associated:

A particular problem arises in the case of cities dominated by branches and subsidiary companies. The performance in the social field of top executives in the head office, where the company has a stronger identity and responsibility to its "home town," usually excels that of heads of subordinate plants and offices in other cities — creating an "absentee" effect. Local managers tend to have less authority, tighter budgets and less local interest and acceptability as "transients on the way to the head office."

Page 21—By FRAZAR B. WILDE:

This is a good statement on a complex subject. It would be in order to include reference to the huge tax payments made by corporations to all political bodies — federal, state, and local.

64.

Page 22—By MARVIN BOWER:

I am concerned that the influence of the current market value for shares and bonus plans geared to short-term profits are shortening the time frame to the disadvantage of the long-term health of the business.

Page 22—By WILLIAM S. EDGERLY:

It is not very useful to debate whether current profitability is a means or an end. There has been no slackening of pressure on the modern manager for current earnings performance. On the contrary, the pressure is heightened by the sensitivity of stock market action to quarterly earnings reports.

Nor is there anything very new about trading off short-run profits in favor of long-run growth. Corporations have been doing this for years when, for example, they spent money for research.

What is significant is the increased sophistication with which these trade-offs are approached. No one doubts that current expenses must be incurred for future growth, but the manager is rated by how well he maintains steady earnings improvement at the same time.

Page 22—By PHILIP SPORN, with which REED O. HUNT has asked to be associated:

This report, more than most documents put out by CED, seems to me to be also flawed by the carelessness of its scholarship. Again and again in the first two chapters, for example, challenging statements are made that simply do not meet any serious test of their veracity. For example, on page 12 the statement is made, "Business has carried out its basic economic responsibilities to society so well largely because of the dynamic workings of the private enterprise system." This is certainly a far too far self-serving declaration. There are many negative features to the performance of business in carrying out its basic economic responsibility, not a word of which is even hinted at in the report.

In chapter 2, page 19, there is a statement that, "The understanding and allegiance of these stockholders is very important because by buying in or selling out they affect the financial standing of the company in the market, its ability to raise capital and acquire other firms, and its general reputation." But I question whether this allegiance of the average stockholder goes so far as to retain and not sell his stock when the latter course serves his own best financial interest.

Once more, on page 21 it is said, "The great growth of corporations in size, market power, and impact on society has naturally brought with it a commensurate growth in responsibilities; in a democratic society, power sooner or later begets equivalent accountability." This can be challenged on several grounds because growth in size also brings with it elephantiasis, arrogance, contempt for law—"the so-called (fill in your own) law."

On page 22 there is a testimonial to the modern professional manager, "The modern professional manager also regards himself, not as an owner disposing of personal property as he sees fit, but as a trustee balancing the interests of many diverse participants and constituents in the enterprise . . ." But the modern professional manager all too often also controls the board—in the words of one of them, "leave the board to me, I can manage them"—and forgets all too soon that in law he is a creature of the board, which is supposed to set his policies. This is just beginning to be recognized but to many perceptive people it has been evident for a long time. Eventually I believe our business laws will catch up in this vacuum of the spelling out of board and management responsibilities but this unqualified testimonial to the modern manager I just do not believe is in broad accord with the facts of life as they exist in business.

Page 23—By MARVIN BOWER:

The primary responsibility for passing this judgment rests with the board of directors.

Page 23—By MARVIN BOWER:

This trend, in my opinion, is not sufficiently pronounced. Directors are often not given sufficient information about the basic health of the business and do not take their responsibilities with sufficient seriousness.

Page 24—By JOSEPH L. BLOCK:

Wise and prudent corporation executives will devote a portion of their time to social responsibilities for all the reasons so well described in this statement; i.e., because such activities can well be in the long-range best interest of their business and "just because it is the right thing to do." And they should do so for another reason, not specifically noted herein.

66.

It is entirely possible that if businessmen were to ignore these responsibilities, government would step in through nationalization or otherwise and the free competitive enterprise system we prize so highly would be lost and with it many of our other cherished freedoms would be in danger. What a high price to pay for indifference or selfishness!

But I would doubt whether, as suggested in the statement, business executives would be justified in discharging social responsibilities to ingratiate themselves and their corporations with financial analysts and enhance the market values of their securities. This would, I believe, be true only in the rarest of cases where a direct and immediate profit from a so-called social action was readily apparent. To achieve these important results they had better rely on the time-tested primary objective of operating an efficient, expanding and profitable business. After all, failing in this, they might as well forget the whole thing for they would have neither the resources, the time, nor perhaps even the business with which to pursue social responsibilities.

Page 24—By PHILIP SPORN, with which REED O. HUNT has asked to be associated:

To elaborate on my earlier criticism of the statement for unqualified testimonials to the modern professional manager and the modern business corporation, I should like to point out that the report goes even further on page 23 in hymning this ode of praise of the modern manager. It says, "The modern management group includes executives who give specialized attention to all the constituencies: employees, stockholders, suppliers, customers, communities, government, the press, and various interest groups." But the modern management group is all too frequently deficient in its understanding of morals and ethics. The late Clarence B. Randall, in his last book, "The Executive in Transition," put it quite succinctly when he said: "The difficulty is that the warning bell of their conscience does not ring as they make their decisions. They plunge into action without pausing to reflect upon the moral implications of the course to which they are committing themselves and their corporations. They have been carefully trained in engineering, cost-accounting, pricing, human relations, and other phases of management, but not in ethics."

And finally, on page 24, again in its extollment of the modern business corporation, the report says, "To be insensitive, even to subtleties, could be disastrous. It becomes necessary for the corporation's own existence that it be highly responsive to the environment in which it lives." All this is fine. The inference that this conveys of a business world that is the best of possible worlds is simply not borne out by the facts of life. It is not borne out by the poisoning wastes released by many of our chemical plants, by the polluting discharges of our pulp and paper mills, by the particulate emissions of many of our power plants, by the smog from the emissions of millions of our badly engineered motor cars. One could go on, but it would merely reenforce a clear attitude of naivete or special pleading on the part of the author or authors, neither of which is defensible in a CED report.

What is even worse, it seems to me, is that it sets up business on a heroic pedestal which I do not think is a good posture for it to assume even if American business operates on higher standards than prevail in any other part of the world. This kind of unrestrained—indeed unmerited —adulation is not going to do it any good, because its deficiencies are still so numerous. If what we are concerned with is fostering business continuing as the single most important item in our social-economic system, then I believe business needs to materially improve its performance in the years ahead.

Page 25—By ROBERT R. NATHAN:

The principal challenge relates to who should resolve the role of business and conflicts with humane values or social environment. Perhaps even more basic is the question of determining what humane values should be pursued and what social environment is desirable.

In a democratic society, subject to constitutional guarantees, the view of the majority should prevail. Commonly we talk of the majority as made up of individuals and not of organizations. Is the corporate entity an appropriate vehicle for representing the divergent and often conflicting interests of its stockholders, management, or even workers concerning such fundamental factors as humane values and social environment?

Given the economic structure of our society and the immense strength and great contributions of corporations in the functioning of our economy, the role of the corporation and of all business in achieving a high quality of life needs the most careful evaluation. What I do find

68.

lacking in this statement is adequate rationale and clarification of the role business should play as a "responsible participant determined to resolve any conflict with humane values or the social environment." It is not enough to call for constructive attitudes and positive contributions. The real question is just how far corporations can or should be expected to go as responsible participants in setting policies or making decisions affecting basic social values. A great many statements in the report are highly illuminating and very constructive and perhaps the issue I am raising calls for a much more thorough approach which CED might continue to pursue in the period ahead.

Page 28—By MARVIN BOWER:

Recognizing the importance to the country and to business of an electorate with a reasonable level of economic literacy, the CED in 1949 joined with the Ford Foundation in establishing the Joint Council on Economic Education, and for a number of years participated with that foundation in financing the Council. The purpose of the Joint Council is to raise the level of economic understanding through increases in the quantity and quality of the economics contents of the curriculums of our schools and colleges and through the training of teachers in economics. The Council is now supported by foundations, business and labor.

Page 28—By ROBERT R. NATHAN, with which E. SHERMAN ADAMS has asked to be associated:

Enlightened self-interest is a highly desirable objective for business but it is not a major alternative to the role of government. It must be recognized that the very nature of a competitive economy renders governmental intervention and regulation not only inevitable but proper. It is not just insensitivity to the changing demands of society which bring pressure for regulation. It is the very essence of vigorous competition which necessitates some authoritative setting down of rules that maximize the fulfillment of public interest.

I agree with the thrust of these observations concerning the desirability of enlightened self-interest but there appears to be some holding out hope of non-regulation if there is business sensitivity to social concerns. The issue is not one of avoiding governmental or social sanctions.

Rather, it is one of not only acquiescing in needed and reasonable regulations, but also of seeking constructive regulations while at the same time objecting to regulations that are more restrictive than necessary.

The exaggeration of there being real alternatives between self-interest and government regulation also is strongly reflected in the last full paragraph on page 30.

Page 30—By WILLIAM H. ABBOTT:

I believe that very few investors in considering whether to purchase or retain a stock consider the effect of that company's social outlays upon his other investments.

Page 32—By WILLIAM S. EDGERLY:

I disagree with the suggestion that traditional measurements of profit be altered, in some unspecified way, to permit diversion of resources into higher priority applications. This suggestion conflicts with the subsequent assertion that return on investment in social markets should be reasonably related to comparable opportunities in traditional lines of business. It is the question of comparability, especially with respect to growth potential and risk, which needs re-examination, not the method of measuring profit.

Page 33—By GEORGE C. McGHEE:

Corporations with healthy earnings and growth prospects should, it is believed, budget progressive annual increases in the percentage of pretax income going to contributions, both totally and to specific categories such as education, urban affairs, culture, etc. in the direction of the limit allowed by law.

Page 36—By RICHARD C. GERSTENBERG:

The first part of chapter 4 raises appropriate questions relative to definition of corporate social involvement. I subscribe to the objectives of the paper as stated in the paragraph following these questions. It is important to stress the fact that the social benefits which society seeks also entail significant costs. These costs deserve our most careful attention and could well have been treated more fully in the policy statement. This issue is complicated by the fact that the measurement of social benefits and social costs presents very difficult methodological and conceptual problems. We do not resolve the measurement issue simply by referring to "reasonable" profits or "reasonable" costs. What do we mean by "reasonable"?

Page 44—By E. SHERMAN ADAMS, with which WILLIAM H. ABBOTT has asked to be associated:

I would heartily agree that voluntary corporate activities to improve the social environment should be expanded and intensified. On the other hand, it is important to appreciate the limitations on what business firms can realistically be expected to accomplish by themselves on complex social problems. Private enterprise unquestionably could and should contribute far more than it has toward solving these problems, but this will not be brought about by preaching, exhortation or wishful thinking. In a competitive, market economy, profit-oriented companies simply cannot devote a really sizable portion of their resources to unprofitable, or even relatively low-profit, activities. Even though businessmen realize that they have a vital stake in the well-being of their communities, there must nevertheless be adequate incentives if the resources of private enterprise are to be mobilized to help deal with social problems on the massive scale that will be required. The most effective way to solve many of these problems is to permit business to earn a reasonable profit for doing much of the work—while at the same time, of course, assessing it for much of the cost by taxing its profits from all its activities.

Page 44—By GEORGE C. McGHEE, with which E. SHERMAN ADAMS has asked to be associated:

Corporate executives, it is believed, fall heir to a personal as well as a corporate responsibility in community affairs, paralleling the importance of the company itself in the total community complex. In many cases, if the top executive does not exercise personal leadership no one else does, or can. Often he alone can give respectability and force to a given project. Although the reverse may on occasion be true and leadership need not always involve the presidency of the local organization involved, the moral and often the convening force of the top company man must be felt.

Page 46—By THOMAS B. McCABE, with which WILLIAM H. ABBOTT has asked to be associated:

The problem of pollution is such a major consideration to the public and of such enormous potential cost that it deserves a far more realistic approach than is conveyed in this statement irrespective of our strong support of the anti-pollution program.

The impact of the problem is very uneven among industries, with some having to bear an almost insurmountable burden while others are relatively free of the problem. Yet, in this administration public officials are loath to make exceptions or grant reasonable tolerances because of the possible political reactions to their acts.

In the area of water pollution, municipalities are major offenders but the public has very little comprehension of the cost of adequate sewage disposal and the extent to which taxes will have to be raised to pay the bill or industrial prices will have to be increased.

Likewise the cost to public utilities. As yet the full impact of the cost factors to the public has not been sufficiently emphasized. Regulatory authorities have been subject to extraordinary change from state and federal administrations, and companies that thought they had forecast their costs under state regulations now find they must increase their projections substantially because of newer regulations.

The problems have become increasingly more complex and the cost of full compliance in some industries may become almost unbearable. Many smaller communities which are economically dependent on a single manufacturing plant may find the cost of anti-pollution compliance is so great that the plant will have to be closed. In such instances the extent of pollution control should be exercised with extraordinary tolerance or the economy of the community will be placed in jeopardy.

It is unrealistic to suppose that industrial companies, even in one-factory communities, will receive the same degree of tolerance as municipalities because of their lack of political or public support and it is these realistic considerations that are not conveyed in the CED statement.

72.

Page 49—By FRANKLIN A. LINDSAY:

The standards suggested here and elsewhere in this statement are commendable but not a satisfactory basis for a company's nonprofit (or less than normal profit) contributions to social purposes.

Where there are several corporate social goals worth pursuing, what criteria should be used in choosing among them? This presumes a limit to how much a company can devote to such activities, which makes choices necessary. How should that limit be determined—by the average ratio of corporate contributions to profits? By the excess of the company's return on net worth over that of competitors?

How should a company's goals for corporate social performance be differentiated from national goals? If "spillover" benefits to non-corporate constituencies exceed benefits to corporate constituencies (of all corporations), shouldn't the goal usually be pursued by government with tax funds or under regulations that apply equally to all competitors? If "spillover" benefits to constituencies of other corporations exceed benefits to a particular company, to what extent should that company pursue the goal by financial support without commitment from other companies to do their share?

When a company chooses to pursue a social goal, there are usually alternative means of doing so. How shall such choices be made—by cost-benefit studies used by government which try to measure benefits to the public or by cost-benefit calculations based upon estimates of corporate benefit, or perhaps by both?

I do not find answers to these questions in the statement, although some are at least suggested. What is needed is more rigorous analytical work in this virtually virgin territory. CED should not stop with this statement, but should pursue these questions further.

Page 52—By THOMAS B. McCABE:

Since labor unions and their leaders are such a vital ingredient in the cooperative effort to attain the goals of American society it would seem that more consideration should be given in this statement to the specific steps that could be taken by them, in concert with the leaders of industry, to attain the desired social goals enumerated by the statement. It is very specific in mentioning the many laudable social areas in which business leaders should be engaged but absent are similar suggestions for the involvement of union leaders.

Page 56—By ROBERT R. NATHAN:

This section does express some of the reasons for being doubtful about major reliance on tax incentives to achieve social objectives. I would go further and suggest that only where other inducements prove to be impractical or ineffective should consideration be given to reliance on tax incentives. Not only is it difficult to apply tax incentives in ways to confine the benefits to those who truly warrant the special help but more serious is the fact that selective tax incentives tend to reduce the tax base and create loopholes and evasions in the tax system.

If our society is to be more responsive to social change and environmental needs, public revenue sources must be maintained and not eroded. I am not against tax incentives in every single instance, but certainly they should be used only where the evidence overwhelmingly indicates large benefits relative to losses in revenues and where there can be assured identifiable relationships between the costs and the benefits.

Page 59—By WILLIAM S. EDGERLY:

This section tends to underplay the importance of private institutions other than business. The role of universities and hospitals in finding new solutions to certain problems, such as the delivery of health care, for example, will rank with that of business.

The statement fails to emphasize the interests and characteristics which business holds in common with other private institutions. One of the most vital of these is the ability to raise and accumulate capital without tax support, which should be included in the list of the best attributes of private enterprise.

CED BOARD OF TRUSTEES

See page 5 for list of Research and Policy Committee
and the Subcommittee members
who are responsible for the conclusions
in this particular study.

Chairman
WILLIAM C. STOLK, Chairman
W. C. Stolk & Associates, Inc.

Vice Chairmen
FRED J. BORCH, Chairman
General Electric Company
JOHN D. HARPER, Chairman of the Board
Aluminum Company of America
ROBERT B. SEMPLE, Chairman
BASF Wyandotte Corporation
THEODORE O. YNTEMA
Department of Economics
Oakland University

Treasurer
WALTER W. WILSON, Partner
Morgan Stanley & Co.

WILLIAM H. ABBOTT
Director and Member of Executive Committee
3M Company
E. SHERMAN ADAMS
Senior Vice President and Economist
The Fidelity Bank
O. KELLEY ANDERSON, Chairman
New England Mutual Life Insurance Company
ROBERT O. ANDERSON
Chairman of the Board
Atlantic Richfield Company
ERNEST C. ARBUCKLE, Chairman
Wells Fargo Bank
ROY L. ASH, President
Litton Industries, Inc.
SANFORD S. ATWOOD, President
Emory University
BERNHARD M. AUER
Executive Vice President
Time Inc.
JERVIS J. BABB
New York, New York
ROBINSON F. BARKER, Chairman
PPG Industries, Inc.
JOSEPH W. BARR, President
American Security and Trust Company
HARRY HOOD BASSETT
Chairman of the Board
First National Bank of Miami
FREDERICK S. BEEBE
Chairman of the Board
Newsweek
WILLIAM S. BEINECKE, Chairman of the Board
The Sperry and Hutchinson Company
S. CLARK BEISE
President (Retired)
Bank of America N.T. & S.A.
GEORGE F. BENNETT, President
State Street Investment Corporation
HAROLD H. BENNETT, President
Zions Cooperative Mercantile Institution
WILLIAM BENTON, Publisher and Chairman
Encyclopaedia Britannica, Inc.
ROBERT BEYER, Managing Partner
Touche Ross & Co.
JOSEPH L. BLOCK
Chairman, Executive Committee
Inland Steel Company
FRED J. BORCH, Chairman
General Electric Company
C. FRED BORDEN
Senior Vice President
Kaiser Industries Corporation
CHARLES P. BOWEN, JR., Chairman
Booz, Allen & Hamilton Inc.
MARVIN BOWER, Director
McKinsey & Company, Inc.
DANIEL P. BRYANT, Chairman
Bekins Company
D. C. BURNHAM, Chairman
Westinghouse Electric Corporation

JOHN L. BURNS, President
John L. Burns and Company
HAROLD BURROW, President
Burrow Enterprises
FLETCHER L. BYROM, Chairman
Koppers Company, Inc.
RAFAEL CARRION, JR.
Chairman and President
Banco Popular de Puerto Rico
EDWARD W. CARTER, President
Broadway-Hale Stores, Inc.
JOHN B. CAVE, Financial Vice President
Burlington Industries, Inc.
HUNG WO CHING, Chairman of the Board
Aloha Airlines, Inc.
W. GRAHAM CLAYTOR, JR., President
Southern Railway System
CATHERINE B. CLEARY, President
First Wisconsin Trust Company
JOHN R. COLEMAN, President
Haverford College
EMILIO G. COLLADO
Executive Vice President
Standard Oil Company (New Jersey)
C. W. COOK, Chairman
General Foods Corporation
JOSEPH COORS
Executive Vice President
Adolph Coors Company
STEWART S. CORT, Chairman
Bethlehem Steel Corporation
ROBERT C. COSGROVE
Chairman of the Board
Green Giant Company
JAMES W. COULTRAP
Consultant, Director
North American Rockwell
GEORGE S. CRAFT, Chairman of the Board
Trust Company of Georgia
JOHN H. DANIELS, Chairman
Archer Daniels Midland Company
*DONALD K. DAVID
New York, New York
ARCHIE K. DAVIS, Chairman of the Board
Wachovia Bank & Trust Co.
FREDERICK B. DENT, President
Mayfair Mills
WILLIAM N. DERAMUS, III
Chairman and President
Kansas City Southern Industries, Inc.
JOHN DIEBOLD, Chairman
The Diebold Group, Inc.
LOWELL S. DILLINGHAM, Chairman
Dillingham Corporation
DOUGLAS DILLON, Chairman
United States and Foreign Securities Corporation
CHARLES E. DUCOMMUN, President
Ducommun Incorporated
H. F. DUNNING, Chairman
Scott Paper Company
ALFRED W. EAMES, JR., Chairman
Del Monte Corporation
W. D. EBERLE, Chairman
American-Standard Inc.
WILLIAM S. EDGERLY
Financial Vice President
Cabot Corporation
LOUIS K. EILERS, Chairman
Eastman Kodak Company
DANIEL F. EVANS, President
L. S. Ayres & Co.
RICHARD C. FENTON, President
Fenton International, Inc.
E. B. FITZGERALD, Chairman
Cutler-Hammer, Inc.
*MARION B. FOLSOM
Rochester, New York
ROBERT T. FOOTE
Chairman of the Board and President
Universal Foods Corporation

*Life Trustee

J. FRANK FORSTER
Chairman and President
Sperry Rand Corporation

WILLIAM C. FOSTER
Washington, D.C.

LAWRENCE E. FOURAKER
Dean, Graduate School of Business
    Administration, Harvard University

JOHN M. FOX, Chairman
United Fruit Company

DAVID L. FRANCIS, Chairman
Princess Coal Sales Company

WILLIAM H. FRANKLIN, President
Caterpillar Tractor Co.

GAYLORD FREEMAN, Chairman of the Board
The First National Bank of Chicago

DON C. FRISBEE, President
Pacific Power & Light Company

CLIFTON C. GARVIN, JR.
Executive Vice President
Standard Oil Company (New Jersey)

RICHARD L. GELB, President
Bristol-Myers Company

RICHARD C. GERSTENBERG
Vice Chairman of the Board
General Motors Corporation

HUGH M. GLOSTER, President
Morehouse College

W. RICHARD GOODWIN, President
Johns-Manville Corporation

KERMIT GORDON, President
The Brookings Institution

LINCOLN GORDON
School of Advanced International Studies

EDWIN H. GOTT, Chairman of the Board
United States Steel Corporation

KATHARINE GRAHAM, Publisher
The Washington Post Company

JOHN D. GRAY, Chairman
Hart Schaffner & Marx

JOHN D. GRAY, Chairman
Omark Industries, Inc.

JOSEPH GRIESEDIECK
Chairman and President
Falstaff Brewing Corporation

WALTER A. HAAS, JR., President
Levi Strauss and Co.

TERRANCE HANOLD, President
The Pillsbury Company

ROBERT V. HANSBERGER
President and Chairman of the Board
Boise Cascade Corporation

JOHN D. HARPER, Chairman of the Board
Aluminum Company of America

SHEARON HARRIS, Chairman and President
Carolina Power & Light Company

WILLIAM E. HARTMANN, Partner
Skidmore, Owings & Merrill

GABRIEL HAUGE, Chairman of the Board
Manufacturers Hanover Trust Company

ELLISON L. HAZARD
Chairman and President
Continental Can Company, Inc.

H. J. HEINZ, II, Chairman
H. J. Heinz Company

JAMES H. HESTER, President
New York University

WILLIAM A. HEWITT, Chairman of the Board
Deere & Company

JAMES T. HILL, JR.
New York, New York

*PAUL G. HOFFMAN, Administrator
United Nations Development Program

REED O. HUNT
Crown Zellerbach Corporation

GEORGE F. JAMES
Dean, Graduate School of Business
Columbia University

WILLIAM M. JENKINS, Chairman of the Board
Seattle-First National Bank

RUSS M. JOHNSON, Chairman
Deposit Guaranty National Bank

SAMUEL C. JOHNSON
Chairman and President
S. C. Johnson & Son, Inc.

WILLIAM B. JOHNSON, Chairman
Illinois Central Industries, Inc.

GILBERT E. JONES, Senior Vice President
IBM Corporation

CHARLES KELLER, JR., President
Keller Construction Corporation

JAMES M. KEMPER, JR., Chairman
Commerce Bank of Kansas City

DONALD M. KENDALL, Chairman of the Board
PepsiCo, Inc.

JAMES R. KENNEDY, Vice Chairman
Celanese Corporation

CHARLES KIMBALL, President
Midwest Research Institute

ROBERT J. KLEBERG, JR., President
King Ranch, Inc.

PHILIP M. KLUTZNICK, Chairman of the Board
Urban Investment and Development Co.

HARRY W. KNIGHT, Chairman of the Board
Knight, Gladieux & Smith, Inc.

SIGURD S. LARMON
New York, New York

RALPH LAZARUS, Chairman of the Board
Federated Department Stores, Inc.

FRANKLIN A. LINDSAY, President
Itek Corporation

WALTER T. LUCKING, Chairman
Arizona Public Service Company

J. EDWARD LUNDY
Executive Vice President
Ford Motor Company

*THOMAS B. McCABE
Chairman, Finance Committee
Scott Paper Company

THOMAS M. McDANIEL, JR., President
Southern California Edison Co.

NEIL McELROY, Chairman
The Procter & Gamble Company

GEORGE C. McGHEE
Washington, D.C.

JOHN D. MacKENZIE
Chairman and President (Retired)
American Smelting & Refining Company

DONALD S. MacNAUGHTON, Chairman
Prudential Insurance Co. of America

G. BARRON MALLORY
P. R. Mallory & Co., Inc.

STANLEY MARCUS, President
Neiman-Marcus Company

AUGUSTINE R. MARUSI
Chairman and President
Borden Inc.

WILLIAM F. MAY, Chairman
American Can Company

OSCAR G. MAYER, JR., Chairman of the Board
Oscar Mayer & Co.

H. TALBOTT MEAD
Chairman, Finance Committee
The Mead Corporation

EDWIN B. MEISSNER, JR.
Senior Vice President
General Steel Industries, Inc.

LOUIS W. MENK, Chairman
Burlington Northern, Inc.

ARJAY MILLER
Dean, Graduate School of Business
Stanford University

BILL D. MOYERS
Garden City, New York

*Life Trustee

RAYMON H. MULFORD, Chairman
Owens-Illinois Inc.

ROBERT R. NATHAN, President
Robert R. Nathan Associates, Inc.

ALFRED C. NEAL, President
Committee for Economic Development

ISIDORE NEWMAN, II, President
City Stores Company

J. WILSON NEWMAN
Chairman, Finance Committee
Dun & Bradstreet, Inc.

JOHN O. NICKLIS
Chairman of the Board
Pitney-Bowes Inc.

EDWARD L. PALMER
Executive Vice President
First National City Bank

HENRY G. PARKS, JR.
President and Chairman of the Board
H. G. Parks, Inc.

HERBERT P. PATTERSON, President
The Chase Manhattan Bank

DeWITT J. PAUL
Beneficial Corporation

DONALD S. PERKINS, President
Jewel Companies, Inc.

JOHN A. PERKINS
Professor of Public Management
Graduate School of Management
Northwestern University

HOWARD C. PETERSEN, Chairman of the Board
The Fidelity Bank

C. WREDE PETERSMEYER
Chairman and President
Corinthian Broadcasting Corporation

RUDOLPH A. PETERSON
Chairman, Executive Committee
Bank of America N.T. & S.A.

GEORGE PUTNAM, Chairman
The Putnam Management Company, Inc.

R. STEWART RAUCH, JR., Chairman
The Philadelphia Saving Fund Society

PHILIP D. REED
New York, New York

JAMES Q. RIORDAN
Senior Vice President, Finance
Mobil Oil Corporation

MELVIN J. ROBERTS, Chairman of the Board
Colorado National Bank of Denver

WILLIAM E. ROBERTS
Chairman and President
Ampex Corporation

JAMES E. ROBISON, Chairman of the Board
Indian Head Inc.

H. I. ROMNES, Chairman and President
American Telephone & Telegraph Company

AXEL G. ROSIN, President
Book-of-the-Month Club, Inc.

WILLIAM M. ROTH
San Francisco, California

CHARLES J. SCANLON, Vice President
General Motors Corporation

THEODORE SCHLESINGER, Chairman
Allied Stores Corporation

JOHN A. SCHNEIDER
Executive Vice President
Columbia Broadcasting System, Inc.

GILBERT H. SCRIBNER, JR., President
Scribner & Co.

ELLERY SEDGWICK, JR., Chairman
Medusa Portland Cement Company

RICHARD B. SELLARS, President
Johnson & Johnson Worldwide

ROBERT B. SEMPLE, Chairman
BASF Wyandotte Corporation

MARK SHEPHERD, JR., President
Texas Instruments Incorporated

LEON SHIMKIN, President
Simon and Schuster, Inc.

GRANT G. SIMMONS, JR., Chairman
Simmons Company

WILLIAM P. SIMMONS, President
Southern Crate & Veneer Co.

DONALD B. SMILEY
Chairman of the Board
R. H. Macy & Co., Inc.

RAYMOND E. SNYDER
Senior Vice President
Merck & Co., Inc.

DAVIDSON SOMMERS, Chairman
The Equitable Life Assurance
   Society of the United States

PHILIP SPORN
New York, New York

ALLAN SPROUL
Kentfield, California

ELVIS J. STAHR, President
National Audubon Society

SYDNEY STEIN, JR., Partner
Stein Roe & Farnham

EDGAR B. STERN, JR., President
Royal Street Corporation

WILLIAM C. STOLK, Chairman
W. C. Stolk & Associates, Inc.

ALEXANDER L. STOTT
Vice President and Comptroller
American Telephone & Telegraph Company

ANNA LORD STRAUSS
New York, New York

ROBERT D. STUART, JR., President
Quaker Oats Company

REV. LEON H. SULLIVAN
Zion Baptist Church

CHARLES P. TAFT
Cincinnati, Ohio

JACKSON W. TARVER, President
Cox Enterprises, Inc.

WALTER N. THAYER, President
Whitney Communications Corporation

WAYNE E. THOMPSON, Senior Vice President
Dayton Hudson Corporation

CHARLES C. TILLINGHAST, JR., Chairman
Trans World Airlines, Inc.

HOWARD S. TURNER, Chairman
Turner Construction Company

L. S. TURNER, JR., President
Dallas Power & Light Co.

ALVIN W. VOGTLE, JR., President
The Southern Company, Inc.

HARRY B. WARNER, President
The B. F. Goodrich Company

ROBERT C. WEAVER
Professor of Economics
The City University of New York

JAMES E. WEBB
Washington, D.C.

SIDNEY J. WEINBERG, JR., Partner
Goldman, Sachs & Co.

HERMAN L. WEISS
Vice Chairman of the Board
General Electric Company

WILLIAM H. WENDEL, President
The Carborundum Company

JOHN H. WHEELER, President
Mechanics and Farmers Bank

*FRAZAR B. WILDE, Chairman Emeritus
Connecticut General Life Insurance Company

*W. WALTER WILLIAMS
Chairman of the Board
Continental, Inc.

JOSEPH C. WILSON, Chairman
Xerox Corporation

WALTER W. WILSON, Partner
Morgan Stanley & Co.

ARTHUR M. WOOD, President
Sears, Roebuck and Co.

THEODORE O. YNTEMA
Department of Economics
Oakland University

*Life Trustee

HONORARY TRUSTEES

CARL E. ALLEN
New York, New York

JAMES L. ALLEN, Honorary Chairman
Booz, Allen & Hamilton, Inc.

FRANK ALTSCHUL
New York, New York

JOHN D. BIGGERS
Perrysburg, Ohio

WALTER R. BIMSON
Chairman Emeritus
Valley National Bank

ROGER M. BLOUGH
White & Case

HAROLD BOESCHENSTEIN
Chairman, Executive Committee
Owens-Corning Fiberglas Corporation

THOMAS D. CABOT
Honorary Chairman of the Board
Cabot Corporation

JAMES V. CARMICHAEL
Smith, Currie & Hancock

EVERETT NEEDHAM CASE
Van Hornesville, New York

FRANK A. CHRISTENSEN
Garden City, New York

WALKER L. CISLER, Chairman
The Detroit Edison Company

PAUL F. CLARK
Boston, Massachusetts

JOHN L. COLLYER
Akron, Ohio

S. SLOAN COLT
New York, New York

JAMES B. CONANT
New York, New York

FAIRFAX M. CONE
Carmel, California

GARDNER COWLES
Chairman of the Board and
    Editorial Chairman
Cowles Communications, Inc.

JAY E. CRANE
New York, New York

JOHN P. CUNNINGHAM
Honorary Chairman of the Board
Cunningham & Walsh, Inc.

PAUL L. DAVIES, Senior Director
FMC Corporation

DONALD C. DAYTON, Director
Dayton Hudson Corporation

ROBERT W. ELSASSER
New Orleans, Louisiana

JAMES A. FARLEY, Chairman of Board
The Coca-Cola Export Corporation

EDMUND FITZGERALD
Milwaukee, Wisconsin

CLARENCE FRANCIS, Director
Economic Development Council of
    New York City, Inc.

ALFRED C. FULLER
West Hartford, Connecticut

PAUL S. GEROT
Honorary Chairman of the Board
The Pillsbury Company

MICHAEL L. HAIDER
New York, New York

ROBERT HELLER
Bratenahl, Ohio

J. V. HERD
Chairman, Investment Committee
The Continental Insurance Companies

OVETA CULP HOBBY
Chairman of the Board
The Houston Post

HENRY R. JOHNSTON
Ponte Vedra Beach, Florida

THOMAS ROY JONES
Consultant, Schlumberger Limited

FREDERICK R. KAPPEL
Retired Chairman of the Board
American Telephone & Telegraph Company

ROY E. LARSEN
Vice Chairman of the Board
Time Inc.

FRED LAZARUS, JR.
Chairman, Executive and Finance Committee
Federated Department Stores, Inc.

DAVID E. LILIENTHAL
President and Chairman
Development and Resources Corporation

ELMER L. LINDSETH
Chairman, Executive Committee
The Cleveland Electric Illuminating Co.

JAMES A. LINEN
Chairman, Executive Committee
Time Inc.

GEORGE H. LOVE
Chairman of the Board
Consolidation Coal Company, Inc.

ROBERT A. LOVETT, Partner
Brown Brothers Harriman & Co.

ROY G. LUCKS, Director
Del Monte Corporation

FRANKLIN J. LUNDING
Chairman, Finance Committee
Jewel Companies, Inc.

L. F. McCOLLUM, Chairman
Continental Oil Company

JOHN A. McCONE
Chairman of the Board
Joshua Hendy Corporation

FOWLER McCORMICK
Chicago, Illinois

FRANK L. MAGEE
Stahlstown, Pennsylvania

JOSEPH A. MARTINO
Honorary Chairman
National Lead Company

JOHN F. MERRIAM
Chairman, Executive Committee
Northern Natural Gas Company

LORIMER D. MILTON, President
Citizens Trust Company

DON G. MITCHELL
Summit, New Jersey

MALCOLM MUIR
Former Chairman of the Board and Editor-in-Chief
Newsweek

AKSEL NIELSEN, Chairman of the Board
Mortgage Investments Co.

JAMES F. OATES, JR., Director
The Equitable Life Assurance
    Society of the United States

W. A. PATTERSON, Retired Chairman
United Air Lines

EDWIN W. PAULEY, Chairman
Pauley Petroleum, Inc.

MORRIS B. PENDLETON
Chairman of the Board Emeritus
Pendleton Tool Industries, Inc.

DONALD C. POWER, Chairman of the Board
General Telephone and
    Electronics Corporation

M. J. RATHBONE
New York, New York

REUBEN B. ROBERTSON
Asheville, North Carolina

RAYMOND RUBICAM
Scottsdale, Arizona

GEORGE RUSSELL
Bloomfield Hills, Michigan

E. C. SAMMONS
Chairman of the Board (Emeritus)
United States National Bank of Oregon

NEIL D. SKINNER, Chairman
Hoffman Specialty Mfg. Corp.

ELLIS D. SLATER
Landrum, South Carolina

DONALD C. SLICHTER
Milwaukee, Wisconsin

S. ABBOT SMITH
Boston, Massachusetts

H. CHRISTIAN SONNE
New York, New York

ROBERT C. SPRAGUE
Chairman of the Board
Sprague Electric Company

ROBERT G. SPROUL, President Emeritus
The University of California

FRANK STANTON, President
Columbia Broadcasting System, Inc.

JOHN P. STEVENS, JR., Director
J. P. Stevens & Co., Inc.

FRANK L. SULZBERGER
Chairman of the Board
Enterprise Paint Mfg. Co.

H. GARDINER SYMONDS, Chairman
Tenneco Inc.

C. A. TATUM, JR., President
Texas Utilities Company

ALAN H. TEMPLE
New York, New York

H. C. TURNER, JR.
Chairman, Executive Committee
Turner Construction Company

ARTHUR B. VAN BUSKIRK
Ligonier, Pennsylvania

J. HUBER WETENHALL, Director
Kraftco Corporation

WALTER H. WHEELER, JR.
Chairman, Executive Committee
Pitney-Bowes Inc.

A. L. WILLIAMS
Chairman, Executive Committee
IBM Corporation

CHARLES E. WILSON
New York, New York

JAMES W. YOUNG
Santa Fe, New Mexico

HARRY W. ZINSMASTER, Chairman
Zinsmaster Baking Company

TRUSTEES ON LEAVE FOR GOVERNMENT SERVICE

CARL J. GILBERT
Special Representative for Trade Negotiations

DAVID M. KENNEDY
Ambassador-at-Large
Department of State

DAVID PACKARD
Deputy Secretary of Defense

DANIEL PARKER
Director at Large
Overseas Private Investment Corporation

PETER G. PETERSON
Executive Director
Council on International Economic Policy

CED PROFESSIONAL AND ADMINISTRATIVE STAFF

ALFRED C. NEAL, *President*

ROBERT F. LENHART
*Vice President
for Research Administration*

FRANK W. SCHIFF
*Vice President
and Chief Economist*

HOWARD P. WHIDDEN
*Vice President
for Publications and Education*

ROBERT F. STEADMAN, *Director*
*Improvement of Management
in Government*

S. CHARLES BLEICH, *Secretary*
Board of Trustees

CHARLES F. ISACKES
Director of Finance
HARVEY M. LEWIS
DAVID B. ROOSEVELT
Assistant Directors

GEORGE T. KLOP, *Comptroller
and Assistant Treasurer*

GEORGE F. FOWLER, *Manager
of Distribution Services*

SOL HURWITZ, *Director
of Information*
JACOB WORENKLEIN
Assistant Director

CARL RIESER, *Editorial
Supervisor*

Research Staff

MARY BALUSS

DONALD R. GILMORE

SEONG PARK

MARY C. MUGIVAN
Publications Coordinator

Statements on National Policy
Issued by the Research
and Policy Committee
(publications in print)

Achieving Energy Independence *(December 1974)*

A New U.S. Farm Policy for Changing World Food Needs *(October 1974)*

Congressional Decision Making for National Security *(September 1974)*

*Toward a New International Economic System:
   A Joint Japanese-American View *(June 1974)*

More Effective Programs for a Cleaner Environment *(April 1974)*

The Management and Financing of Colleges *(October 1973)*

Strengthening the World Monetary System *(July 1973)*

Financing the Nation's Housing Needs *(April 1973)*

Building a National Health-Care System *(April 1973)*

*A New Trade Policy Toward Communist Countries *(September 1972)*

High Employment Without Inflation:
   A Positive Program for Economic Stabilization *(July 1972)*

Reducing Crime and Assuring Justice *(June 1972)*

Military Manpower and National Security *(February 1972)*

The United States and the European Community *(November 1971)*

Improving Federal Program Performance *(September 1971)*

Social Responsibilities of Business Corporations *(June 1971)*

Education for the Urban Disadvantaged:
   From Preschool to Employment *(March 1971)*

Statements issued in association with CED counterpart organizations in foreign countries.

Further Weapons Against Inflation *(November 1970)*

Making Congress More Effective *(September 1970)*

*Development Assistance to Southeast Asia *(July 1970)*

Training and Jobs for the Urban Poor *(July 1970)*

Improving the Public Welfare System *(April 1970)*

Reshaping Government in Metropolitan Areas *(February 1970)*

Economic Growth in the United States *(October 1969)*

Assisting Development in Low-Income Countries *(September 1969)*

*Nontariff Distortions of Trade *(September 1969)*

Fiscal and Monetary Policies for Steady Economic Growth *(January 1969)*

Financing a Better Election System *(December 1968)*

Innovation in Education: New Directions for the American School *(July 1968)*

Modernizing State Government *(July 1967)*

*Trade Policy Toward Low-Income Countries *(June 1967)*

How Low Income Countries Can Advance Their Own Growth *(September 1966)*

Modernizing Local Government *(July 1966)*

A Better Balance in Federal Taxes on Business *(April 1966)*

Budgeting for National Objectives *(January 1966)*

Presidential Succession and Inability *(January 1965)*

Educating Tomorrow's Managers *(October 1964)*

Improving Executive Management in the Federal Government *(July 1964)*

Trade Negotiations for a Better Free World Economy *(May 1964)*

Union Powers and Union Functions: Toward a Better Balance *(March 1964)*

Japan in the Free World Economy *(April 1963)*

Economic Literacy for Americans *(March 1962)*

Cooperation for Progress in Latin America *(April 1961)*

Statements issued in association with CED counterpart organizations in foreign countries.

BCL-3rded.

TEXAS A&M UNIVERSITY-TEXARKANA